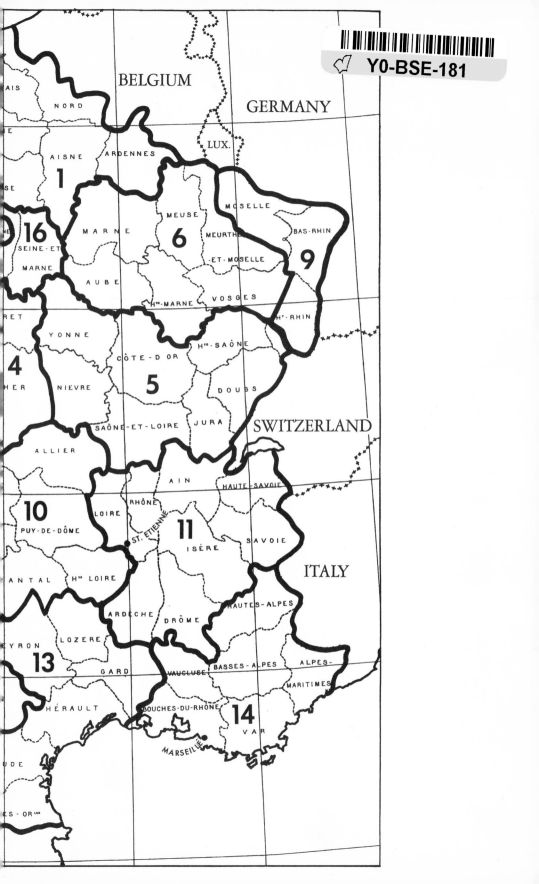

Monographs

of the Rutgers Center of Alcohol Studies

No. 5

Monographs of the
Rutgers Center of Alcohol Studies

Under the editorship of Mark Keller

This monograph series was begun as "Monographs of the Yale Center of Alcohol Studies" and Numbers 1, 2 and 3 in the series were published at Yale. Beginning with Number 4 the series has been continued as Monographs of the Rutgers Center of Alcohol Studies. The change conforms with the transfer of the Center from Yale to Rutgers University. The works published in this series report the results of original research in any of the scientific disciplines, whether performed at Rutgers or elsewhere.

No. 1. Alcohol and the Jews. A Cultural Study of Drinking and Sobriety. By CHARLES R. SNYDER. $5.00

No. 2. Revolving Door. A Study of the Chronic Police Case Inebriate. By DAVID J. PITTMAN and C. WAYNE GORDON. $4.00

No. 3. Alcohol in Italian Culture. Food and Wine in Relation to Sobriety among Italians and Italian Americans. By GIORGIO LOLLI, EMIDIO SERIANNI, GRACE M. GOLDER and PIERPAOLO LUZZATTO-FEGIZ. $4.00

No. 4. Drinking among Teen-Agers. A Sociological Interpretation of Alcohol Use by High-School Students. By GEORGE L. MADDOX and BEVODE C. McCALL. $6.00

No. 5. Drinking in French Culture. By ROLAND SADOUN, GIORGIO LOLLI and MILTON SILVERMAN. $6.00

Drinking in French Culture

Distributed by

COLLEGE & UNIVERSITY PRESS · *Publishers*

263 CHAPEL STREET   NEW HAVEN, CONN.

Drinking in French Culture

BY

ROLAND SADOUN

Director, French Institute of Public Opinion, Paris

GIORGIO LOLLI, M.D.

*Director, International Center for Psychodietetics
New York and Rome*

AND

MILTON SILVERMAN, Ph.D.

*Director of Medical Research, Wine Advisory Board
California State Department of Agriculture, San Francisco*

PUBLICATIONS DIVISION
RUTGERS CENTER OF ALCOHOL STUDIES
NEW BRUNSWICK   NEW JERSEY

Copyright © 1965 by
Journal of Studies on Alcohol, Incorporated
New Brunswick, New Jersey

Library of Congress catalog card number: 65-22389

2108

MANUFACTURED IN THE UNITED STATES OF AMERICA BY
UNITED PRINTING SERVICES, INC.
NEW HAVEN, CONN.

Contents

List of Tables

Acknowledgments

Grateful appreciation is expressed to the French High Committee for Study and Information on Alcoholism for the use of hitherto unpublished data on the consumption of beverages and on popular attitudes toward alcohol, and especially to Professor Robert Debré, President of the High Committee, to Alain Barjot, Counsellor to the State, who served as Secretary General of the High Committee until 1962, and to Léon Fleck, his successor, for their continuing advice and warm support.

Appreciation is likewise extended to Dr. Jean Stoetzel, Professor of Social Psychology at the University of the Sorbonne and Director of the Center for Sociological Research, who served as President of the French Institute of Public Opinion (IFOP), and to the psychologists, sociologists, statisticians, and survey teams of IFOP for their invaluable cooperation.

Finally, thanks are extended to the Department of Agriculture of the State of California for financial support which made portions of this research possible.

Introduction

THE STUDY OF DRINKING as a form of human behavior interesting in its own right was advocated by Selden D. Bacon more than twenty years ago. Sociologists and psychologists en masse failed to see the point. The few investigations of the drinking ways of selected groups that emerged in the past generation were hinged on the interest in drunken behavior. If the drinking ways of some ethnic or nationality groups came under formal scrutiny it was because they were either surprisingly free of alcoholism or ostensively given to drunkenness. Essentially this state of affairs has not changed. To justify research on drinking, it is still thought necessary to note that the knowledge gained will help to explain some antisocial or pathological effects.

DRINKING IN FRENCH CULTURE is by no means a pure exception. It could properly have been titled "Drinking and Drunkenness" or "Drinking and Alcoholism" etc. That it bears only the shorter title suggests the authors' recognition of the significance of drinking itself as a social phenomenon worthy of systematic study. They are aware that much as the concern over alcoholism may have motivated the support of their inquiry, its chief contribution is "a fuller understanding of the place of . . . drinking in French culture."

French drinking in particular has literally been screaming for systematic investigation, but the need has been—it is tempting to say, systematically—ignored. Yet if drinking is everywhere surrounded by gossip and misrepresentation, French drinking customs seem even more beclouded by fable and fiction. The present book is thus an urgently needed start at facing facts. As the bibliography indicates, a number of workers in France—outstandingly Bastide, Bresard, Ledermann and Stoetzel—began several years ago to take a realistic look at the national drinking picture, gathering and organizing facts instead of reiterating the traditional cri d'alarme. Except for Ledermann's splendid book, much of the valuable information which they accumulated, largely under the stimulus of the Haut Comité d'Etude et d'Information sur l'Alcoolisme, has regrettably remained obscure in limited reportage. Hopefully the publication of the present work, which takes account of important segments of those investigations, will rectify this situation.

No one can doubt the importance of comparative studies of drinking—and drunkenness too—in different countries and cultures. From this viewpoint the addition of the present gallery of pictures from France to others in this series is decidedly welcome. These others include the drinking practices of Italians, Americans of Italian extraction, American Jews, and American teen-agers.

In the present book, a series of studies first begun late in 1956 attempt to describe "all the drinking in France," covering herb tea and hot chocolate as well as cider, wines and hard liquors. Popular and medical attitudes toward drinking are then detailed. Next, an outstandingly important survey depicts the drinking patterns of the entire French population from childhood through adulthood. What they drank and drink is reported, how much and how often and where and in what connections, and also when and how they started, when they first drank too much, and how often they have drunk too much. Never has so much information been assembled about the drinking of an entire nation, stratified by sex and age, occupation and education, region and community size. And finally, an investigation of the drinking of French alcoholics is reported—not, this time, with a true sample, yet giving a picture that is far from fiction.

That this work rests on a multilayered foundation of statistics is obvious. The question will be asked, how useful are some of these statistics, now approaching ten years in age? There is a curious attitude toward statistics—perhaps fostered by popular journalism—that only "the latest figures" are worthy of attention. An estimate, say, of the rate of alcoholism in a certain year—would that it were right within 20%—results the next year in a demand for a new estimate—"but those figures are last year's, aren't they?"—although the chances that the rate would have changed by as much as 1% are infinitesimal. The fact is that by the time the printer's ink dries on a statistic, it is dead! If the exact rate and the exact number were important, we would have to do nothing but sit and calculate interminably. They are not important. When one of the present surveys was made, it came out that 14% of the women drank 55% of all the alcohol drunk by women in France. It could be that today, as this is written, 15% of the women drank 56% of all the alcohol; or today, when this is read, 16% of the women drank 54%. It doesn't matter. What matters is that a small segment of the population—men as well as women—drinks an enormously disproportionate share of the alcohol; and this condition, even if it is undergoing change, as the present report suggests, will have altered only a little bit. The sole advantage in newer statistics would be not in the exact more recent percentages but in revealing the direction of change. Thus continued surveying and updating are desirable, but the present statistics are not invalidated by a moderate aging. They are, in fact, new, and give a valid picture of drinking and drunkenness in France.

If this book does nothing more than begin the end of fictioneering about French drinking, it will deserve the everlasting gratitude of all students of the facts of life. Some thirty years ago, as a beginning observer of the phenomena of alcoholism in America, I was told that in France things were different: "The French don't have any alcoholism, because they drink wine." Periodically during the next twenty years I was treated to the same pronouncement by earnest clichétists. In the meantime I had learned a few facts, so when asked by an interviewer from one of those weeklies whose readers like to think of them as news magazines to tell them something new, I did: It's not true that the French have no alcoholism because they drink wine; they have more alcoholism than 'most anybody, and besides drinking more wine they also drink more hard liquor than any other people. The next week this periodical published the news: "The French don't have any alcoholism because they drink wine." Well remembered too is the repeated depiction of "the typical French drinker"—sitting for hours at a little round table outside his favorite café on the Boulevard, sipping his one petit-verre while reading the day's papers or ogling the passing girls. Actually I doubted this story even the first time I heard it, but by the tenth time it was beginning to impress me. This Boulevardier type apparently went underground during the war, and has been replaced by the "inveterate" French drinker who is typically never without some alcohol in his system, day in, night out. No doubt there were—maybe there still are—such seasoned Boulevardiers; and no doubt the inveterate drinkers exist too. But as "types" they may be fictions—at least no one has counted their number or measured their drinking. What the drinking of the French—and of many segments of the French—is really like is reported in vast and fascinating detail in this book. Perhaps one of those "news" magazines will not report that the gist of this book is that "the French have no alcoholism because they drink wine."

Undoubtedly the comparison of the findings in France with those in Italy is one of the plus values of the present work. Certain similarities in the wine culture of these neighboring countries, as well as some rather superficial resemblances of the people, would lead to the expectation of like drinking patterns and drinking effects. In both countries wine is consumed copiously by the entire population, and children are initiated early into the drinking custom. But there the similarity stops and one country seems relatively free of problems associated with drinking while the other seems burdened by a gross excess of drunkenness and alcoholism.

Comparisons such as those attempted here have other values which, if not immediately apparent, will emerge as the study of these problems advances and gains sophistication. Thus, the attitude part of the present investigation reveals that French physicians who recognize that a severe alcoholism problem exists, assign the most superficial reasons for it—such as "difficult living and working conditions, poor housing, low standards of living" in the working class, and "fashionable drinking at social affairs" in the upper classes. But the conditions of workers in Italy are not essentially better, and upper class Italians are as fashionable as anybody. Recognition that they have far less drinking pathologies than the French may suggest the need of a deeper search for causes. (The assignment of superficial "causes," however, is not a specialty of French physicians; this is an international and interprofessional practice.)

The "inveterate" drinker "type" has, incidentally, prompted the notion that French alcoholism is caused by alcoholization—supposedly differing in this respect from, for example, American alcoholism. If the study of causation goes deep enough, it may advance to the question whether some Frenchmen become alcoholics because they drink so much, or drink so much because they are fit to become alcoholics. Surely the native drinking patterns may be responsible for allowing the greatest number of the vulnerable—as E. M. Jellinek suggested—to become alcoholics. But just as surely, it is the vulnerable who drink enough to become alcoholics. And just as surely, the drinking customs might be dyssocial even if they did not cause an obtrusively high rate of alcoholism.

The highest value of this work, then, is precisely in what its authors have claimed—in allowing a better understanding of the place of drinking in French culture. Since there are 44 tables, many of them quite elaborate, it may seem to be a statistical work. That is not the point. Since the information is categorized by sex, age, residence, education, marital status, and other "sociocultural" traits, it may seem to be a sociological work. That is not the point either. This is in fact an anthropological essay, except that the subjects are not preliterate Tarachirinuk but the modern French. Of course it is not a complete anthropological work; but it is the necessary foundation for the anthropology of French drinking.

To say that its highest value is in illuminating the place of drinking in a culture, however, is not to deny that this book exposes also the painful issue of alcoholism—an issue that the authors by no means have sought to evade. Their final word, in fact, is devoted to the question of the prevention of alcoholism. They conclude—on grounds reasonably related to their facts—that it is drunkenness, or ways of drinking that permit getting drunk, which must be prevented. Recognizing that drinking is there to stay, they would aim at a modification of the customs so as to inhibit intoxication. Education, they believe, applied especially at the adolescent juncture, would work—but education that would recognize the positive aspects of moderate drinking, especially according to the Italian model, while hitting at all forms of drinking favorable to excess.

A successful reform of drinking customs which would avert inebriety, would prevent more evils than alcoholism. That education alone can do it, however, remains to be demonstrated. Some reform of the regulations of alcoholic beverages might help too, or might speed the process. One suspects that historical changes in the course of the nation, which have nothing directly to do with drinking, will also have some influence on drinking ways and on the rate of recourse to alcoholism. But there is no question that the recommendations of the authors are sound. The proposal to try to educate French boys and girls to drink only moderately and only in circumstances that favor moderation seems to be reasonable and appropriate.

One wishes to believe in the power of education to persuade youth to do what is good for them and for their country. But education is a word of many meanings. In the United States education about the dangers of drinking took the form of preachments which were largely ineffective. The mere difference that the purpose will be to promote moderation instead of abstinence will hardly be enough. More truly educative methods, education that will appeal to youth as more than propaganda from above, will need to be devised. If the French can develop that sort of education, the world will eagerly learn from them.

MARK KELLER

Chapter 1

ALL THE DRINKING IN FRANCE

1. Introduction

THE SERIES of related investigations to be reported here, begun in 1956 and extended over several years, involved a large number of people, including several samples representing the entire adult population of France. One of the goals was a clarification of some of the factors related to the problem of alcoholism. Another and more far-reaching purpose was a fuller understanding of the place of alcohol, or drinking, in French culture.

From the outset, it was decided that the investigation should not be limited to any one beverage or even only to all alcoholic beverages. Instead, the survey was designed to include all beverages, and to examine the use of beverages—especially of those containing alcohol—in relation to the use of solid food.

In the past, dietary surveys and routine nutritional investigations have generally ignored beverages, except milk. Other fluids, from water and coffee to wine, beer and distilled spirits, have apparently been dismissed as unimportant.[1] Nevertheless the nutritional and psychological significance of all these beverages is substantial and may have an influence even greater than that of many solid foods on the health of an individual and the welfare of his family and his community.

Whether or not they contain alcohol, beverages are foods in liquid form. They contribute to the homeostatic regulation of the body and are indispensable participants in the fundamental processes of metabolism. Their nutritional value is obvious and can usually be described in the standard terms of calories, proteins, vitamins, minerals and the like. Their study is vital to the nutritionist.

In the same way, the study of beverages is also vital to the student of behavior and social phenomena. Each major beverage has deep and important emotional meanings, the consumption of these liquid

[1] Keller (20) has called attention to the Bureau of Home Economics survey of the national diet (55) in the 1930s, in which alcoholic beverages were completely ignored, as if they did not exist and did not substantially influence the American dietary. In a more recent repetition of this survey (56), however, alcoholic beverages were taken into account as fully as tomato juice and cola drinks.

1

food items is governed in considerable part by psychosocial determinants, and the use of certain beverages under certain conditions may be either beneficial or fraught with danger to the individual and his society. The psychosocial values of beverages are clearly apparent, exemplified by the emotional significance of milk in the earliest mother–child relationships, the religious symbolism of wine, the ritual of the simmering coffee-pot awaiting the visitor, the sharing of carbonated beverages by children and adolescents, and the individual and collective nonreligious uses of all alcoholic beverages.

Such beverage uses, however, cannot be studied effectively apart from the eating of solid food. Eating and drinking are two closely related facets of the process of nutrition. Once the infant has outgrown its exclusively liquid diet, the ties between eating and drinking are close. In some cultures these ties remain indissoluble throughout life; adults invariably drink when they eat and eat when they drink. In others, these associations may be radically changed; adults will always drink when they eat but will not always eat when they drink.

These and other cultural patterns, which probably derive from factors in early life, may be involved in excessive drinking, in alcohol intoxication, and in alcohol addiction. They are reflected in the attitudes toward drinking of French adults, as well as in their drinking habits, which will be described hereinafter.[2]

METHOD OF SURVEY

The interviews were conducted by the French Institute of Public Opinion (IFOP) between October 1956 and January 1957, by 19 interviewers of both sexes. These interviewers were supervised by 3 staff members of IFOP.

Each respondent was asked to indicate what foods and beverages of any sort he had consumed only during the previous 24 hours. The data, therefore, may serve only to indicate a 24-hour consumption; they may not be used to indicate the average daily intake over an entire year. Further, since the study was conducted during a limited number of months, seasonal changes in intake cannot be deduced. For example, the consumption of aperitifs, notably anisette aperitifs, undoubtedly changes from one season to another; the same can be said of beer, cider, wine and even brandy, which is probably consumed in larger quantities during the colder months.

During the interview, each respondent was asked to describe the

[2] A preliminary account of certain of these findings has been presented elsewhere by Stoetzel (48, p. 61).

nature of the beverage or food consumed and to estimate the quantities. He was also asked to describe where the consumption took place and with what companions.

Precautions were taken, in anticipation of possible defensiveness by persons questioned about drinking, to embody the use of alcoholic beverages within the framework of a more general study of the use of all food. Every effort was made to avoid alerting the respondents to the special interest of the survey in alcohol and thus, as far as possible, to avert evasiveness.

The respondents were selected so as to comprise a stratified sample of the adult population of France (aged 21 and over). It is probable, therefore, with the qualifications indicated above, that the findings represent the general practices of the French people.

Description of Sample

Sex. The 3,005 respondents consisted of 49% men and 51% women.

Age. Classified by age, the respondents were divided as follows: less than 30 years, 22%; 30–39, 22%; 40–49, 17%; 50–59, 18%; 60–69, 13%; and 70 or over, 8%.

Education. Approximately 73% of the men and 76% of the women had completed only primary school (6 years); 6% of the men and 8% of the women had completed upper primary school (8 years); 9% of the men and 6% of the women had studied in a technical school (8 years); 6% of the men and 6% of the women had studied in a secondary school (12 years); 4% of the men and 2% of the women had attended college. No information was available from 2%.

Occupation. The occupations of the respondents, given as that of the head of the family, were as follows: farm owners, 16%; farm workers, 6%; businessmen or shopkeepers, 12%; professionals or executives, 4%; white-collar workers, 10%; manual laborers or domestics, 37%; housewives, retired or no profession, 15%.

Economic Group. The respondents were classified according to their standard of living as follows: wealthy, 6%; well-to-do, 31%; modest, 46%; poor, 13%; no information, 4%. These divisions were based on an arbitrary classification involving ownership of property, ownership of an automobile, ownership of a radio, and employment of domestic servants.

Residence. Approximately 37% lived in communities with a population of less than 2,000; 13%, 2,000 to 5,000; 17%, 5,000 to 20,000; 16%, 20,000 to 100,000; and 17% in the largest communities, with a population of 100,000 or more.

Region. The study was conducted in 305 localities, including all the departments in France except Lot, Loiret, Hautes-Pyrenées, Hautes-Alpes and Corsica. The regional distribution of respondents, which will be described in more detail below, corresponded closely to the national population distribution.

2. TOTAL FLUIDS

Fluids are obviously essential components of the diet, required for the maintenance of the internal environment of the individual and for his very survival. It is necessary, therefore, to consider the ingestion of total fluids, both alcoholic and nonalcoholic. In addition, a curious relationship has been suggested between the total fluid consumption of a cultural group and its susceptibility to alcohol addiction: Italians have both a low rate of alcoholism and a limited intake of total fluids, while Italian Americans show both an increasing use of total fluids and a rising incidence of excessive drinking of alcoholic beverages (34, *p. 44*). Observations of known alcoholics have likewise indicated that they are also excessive drinkers of fluids in general.[3]

During the preceding 24 hours, the Frenchman's average consumption was approximately 1,150 cc. of all forms of beverages, alcoholic as well as nonalcoholic; while that of the Frenchwoman was approximately 720 cc. The average intakes by the various population categories are shown in Tables 1 and 2.

Alcoholic beverages accounted for 61% of the total fluid intake of the men, and approximately 27% of the women's intake. Among both men and women the total intake of beverages was approximately the same in each population category except those who had retired from active vocational life.

In the various age groups, a drastic reduction in the consumption of alcoholic beverages is clearly apparent among the older respondents. Relatively high amounts of alcoholic beverages were consumed by farm workers of both sexes, and there was a decreasing amount of alcohol consumption with increasing education. No clear relationship is evident between the percentage of total fluid consumed as alcoholic beverages and either economic status or residence.

While the average total fluid consumption of the French was nearly 1,000 cc. per day, it is interesting to note that among Italian adults the daily average is less than 900 cc. per day (34, *p. 44*).

3. NONALCOHOLIC BEVERAGES

It has already been stated that the use of food items in liquid form has not only nutritional significance but also psychosocial implications which may be equally important and which vary con-

[3] LOLLI, G. [Unpublished Observations, Yale Plan Clinic, New Haven, Conn., and Knickerbocker Hospital, New York City.]

TABLE 1.—*Average Per Capita Consumption of Alcoholic and Nonalcoholic Beverages in 24 Hours, by Population Categories (Men)*

| | Alc. | | Nonalc. | | Total |
	cc.	%	cc.	%	cc.
Total	708	61	444	39	1152
Age (years)					
Under 30	766	61	491	39	1257
30–39	828	65	450	35	1278
40-49	746	63	440	37	1186
50–59	767	66	392	34	1159
60–69	436	51	418	49	854
70+	384	47	440	53	824
Occupation					
Farm owners	813	69	369	31	1182
Farm workers	953	73	344	27	1297
Business owners	686	62	426	38	1112
Professional, Executives	623	52	575	48	1198
White collar	547	52	499	48	1046
Manual	798	64	452	36	1250
Retired	347	43	454	57	801
Education					
Primary	694	62	420	38	1114
Upper Primary	777	65	416	35	1193
Technical	646	56	503	44	1149
Secondary	538	50	541	50	1079
College	434	43	566	57	1000
Economic Group					
Wealthy	732	58	537	42	1269
Well-to-do	664	60	450	40	1114
Modest	723	62	439	38	1162
Poor	812	68	387	32	1199
Residence (population)					
Under 2,000	755	66	388	34	1143
2,000–5,000	687	62	429	38	1116
5,000–20,000	660	59	465	41	1125
20,000–100,000	671	57	499	43	1170
Over 100,000	699	59	478	41	1177

siderably according to the beverage. This is particularly true of water, milk and coffee or tea.

Some facetious French commentators have suggested that water is uncivilized, unsuitable and particularly unpalatable for human consumption, and should be used only for navigation, fire-fighting and bathing. More serious writers have observed that many Frenchmen think and act as if water were not able to quench thirst (37, *p. 60*). Nevertheless it appears that water has always been accepted

TABLE 2.—*Average Per Capita Consumption of Alcoholic and Nonalcoholic Beverages in 24 Hours, by Population Categories (Women)*

	Alc.		Nonalc.		Total
	cc.	%	cc.	%	cc.
Total	191	27	528	73	719
Age (years)					
Under 30	216	29	531	71	747
30–39	208	28	531	72	739
40–49	196	28	510	72	706
50–59	212	28	540	72	752
60–69	134	20	529	80	663
70+	89	15	513	85	602
Occupation					
Farm owners	244	32	514	68	758
Farm workers	264	33	525	67	789
Business owners	216	29	521	71	737
White collar	193	28	499	72	692
Laborers, domestics	221	29	536	71	757
Retired, housewives	165	24	535	76	700
Education					
Primary	196	28	504	72	700
Upper Primary	160	24	507	76	667
Technical	191	25	563	75	754
Secondary	109	17	549	83	658
College	126	17	605	83	731
Economic Group					
Wealthy	224	30	522	70	746
Well-to-do	182	26	520	74	702
Modest	183	25	535	75	718
Poor	178	26	508	74	686
Residence (population)					
Under 2,000	195	28	499	72	694
2,000–5,000	206	28	542	72	748
5,000–20,000	183	26	534	74	717
20,000–100,000	181	25	540	75	721
Over 100,000	186	25	565	75	751

as a beverage by at least some Frenchmen, and it is unquestionably so used today.

But the use and availability of water have important special implications. The distressing experience of thirst—from which few escape during their lifetimes—often leads to anxiety lest water be even temporarily unavailable. Thus, while solid food is rarely required in the bedroom, water is often kept within comforting reach. In the United States, water coolers are almost ubiquitous, as a symbol of a need which should be satisfied without delay. The teacher's and orator's anxiety is allayed by the glass of water on the desk or stand.

Recent health-education campaigns in some countries have tended to place heavy emphasis on dietary minerals, proteins, vitamins and other biochemical factors. As a result, in the United States, for example, knowledge of the high nutritional value of milk, coupled with the general availability of refrigeration, has made this food acceptable to adults as well as children. But in France, Italy and other countries the situation is usually different. Although the values of milk are appreciated, they are believed to apply primarily to infant nutrition. Lack of refrigeration facilities—except in the larger cities —has made it difficult or impossible to provide milk at a temperature acceptable to adults. Accordingly, milk drinking by adults is often construed as childish behavior.

The very early use of milk is intimately involved in the adequacy or inadequacy of the mother–child relationship, which may be reflected later in the shaping of adult drinking habits. Suttie (50), for example, has declared that inadequacies in the mother–child relationship contribute to the origins of what he called the "taboo on tenderness," the more or less marked inhibition of the powerful urge to express and share warm and tender feelings. Expression and sharing of these feelings greatly contribute to the adult individual's psychosocial adequacy. The latter may include the ability to regulate the intake of alcohol. On the other hand, inhibition of warm and tender feelings seems to contribute, at least in part, to alcoholic excesses.

The psychosocial values of coffee and tea as beverages have been almost universally appreciated. In nearly every country, and in nearly every socioeconomic group, the offer of a cup of coffee or tea is translated immediately as the offer of hospitality and friendship.

Any consideration of the uses of such beverages therefore requires an appreciation not only of the quantities drunk, and the amounts of vitamins, minerals, fats, proteins and carbohydrates included, but also of their psychological and social values.

Water

The data in Table 3 provide no support for the stereotyped belief that all Frenchmen drink only wine and avoid water as a potentially contaminated or otherwise uncivilized beverage. During the preced-

TABLE 3.—*Water Consumption in 24 Hours: Percentage of Users and Average Consumption (cc.) per User, by Population Categories*

| | PLAIN WATER | | | | MINERAL WATER | | | |
| | % of Users | | Consumption | | % of Users | | Consumption | |
	Men	Women	Men	Women	Men	Women	Men	Women
Total	23	44	225	186	11	17	272	202
Age (years)								
Under 30	26	47	254	216	9	12	333	240
30–39	24	44	249	187	10	17	283	199
40–49	18	42	198	170	10	15	236	194
50–59	19	38	210	209	12	22	244	208
60–69	32	43	205	164	11	20	231	174
70+	24	49	180	122	11	15	296	175
Occupation								
Farm owners	18	45	278	174	2	6	280	120
Farm workers	15	47	191	181	1	6	300	150
Businessmen	23	38	228	191	17	26	263	196
Professional, Executives	34		197		30		237	
White collar	38	45	257	198	15	19	265	230
Manual	20	46	228	203	9	24	291	207
Retired	30	44	172	182	16	15	261	206
Education								
Primary	20	43	209	179	9	14	272	201
Upper Primary	30	42	200	210	7	32	217	158
Technical	35	55	275	231	10	15	267	150
Secondary	28	43	288	182	16	28	320	258
College	33	52	257	209	30	29	258	294
Economic Group								
Wealthy	27	38	248	224	26	23	286	192
Well-to-do	23	46	218	180	10	17	253	165
Modest	24	42	230	191	10	17	289	219
Poor	21	51	213	171	5	7	267	189
Residence (population)								
Under 2,000	19	42	221	179	4	10	230	155
2,000–5,000	26	38	199	189	6	15	250	245
5,000–20,000	21	43	202	179	15	19	292	203
20,000–100,000	28	50	233	191	15	19	275	219
Over 100,000	28	44	258	200	18	27	275	209

ing 24 hours, 23% of the men and 44% of the women drank plain or unbottled water, while 11% of the men and 17% of the women drank mineral or bottled water.

Invariably, in each population group, water was used by a higher proportion of women than men. In general, plain water was most commonly accepted by the very young and very old, by the most educated, by the wealthy, and by the inhabitants of larger communities.

An even more marked preference for mineral water was demonstrated by members of the higher economic groups and by residents of larger cities. This is probably a reflection of the cost of this beverage, as well as a testimonial to the supposed healing powers of mineral water and a long-standing belief in many European groups that it has great value in the treatment of "liver disease," indigestion and a host of other real or imaginary disorders.

Among the middle-age groups—those between 40 and 59—the decreased popularity of plain water was balanced by an increased popularity of mineral water.

The average quantity drunk by each man was 225 cc. of plain water and 272 cc. of mineral water, and by each woman, 186 cc. and 202 cc. Most of the plain water and nearly all the mineral water was consumed at home, rather than at a café or restaurant. Similarly, most was taken with lunch rather than with breakfast or dinner or between meals.

Milk

Like other Mediterranean people, the French have long viewed milk as a suitable and even essential food for the very young and the very old. It has not been so accepted for most adults. This is evident in the respondents. Only 6% of the men and 7% of the women reported drinking any plain milk—as distinct from coffee with milk—during the preceding 24 hours. Among those who drank milk, men on the average drank 427 cc. and women 264.

As shown in Table 4, the highest percentage of milk drinkers was among older men and women. A relatively high consumption was reported by men in the upper economic groups. No trends are apparent by occupation—except for a higher percentage of users among retired men—or by education or residence.

Most of the French milk drinkers took this beverage at home—usually at breakfast—rather than at a café, restaurant or bar. Evidently few Frenchmen go to a bar to drink milk.

It may be noted that this survey was conducted 3 years after former Premier Mendès-France inaugurated his campaign to stimulate milk consumption by adults, and 4 years before French newspapers and other media of information began stressing the possible

TABLE 4.—*Milk Consumption in 24 Hours: Percentage of Users and Average Consumption (cc.) per User, by Population Categories*

	% of Users		Consumption	
	Men	Women	Men	Women
Total	6	7	427	264
Age (years)				
Under 30	7	6	400	369
30–39	4	7	400	172
40–49	5	5	540	240
50–59	5	8	420	263
60–69	9	8	289	263
70+	13	17	431	470
Occupation				
Farm owners	6	9	533	256
Farm workers	7	12	601	292
Businessmen	6	5	201	220
Professional, Executives	4		200	
White collar	5	6	181	267
Manual	5	7	480	172
Retired	11	8	373	288
Education				
Primary	5	7	480	286
Upper Primary	7	13	243	246
Technical	11	7	291	314
Secondary	8	2	401	199
College	8	10	112	110
Economic Group				
Wealthy	11	8	191	188
Well-to-do	6	5	467	280
Modest	6	8	367	288
Poor	4	8	775	212
Residence (population)				
Under 2,000	5	8	580	213
2,000–5,000	6	10	451	310
5,000–20,000	6	7	200	271
20,000–100,000	7	6	501	350
Over 100,000	7	7	300	257

relationship between milk fats and coronary disease or atherosclerosis.

Although it might be tempting to infer relationship between the limited use of milk and the relatively high rate of alcoholism in France, it should be recalled that in Italy a low adult consumption of milk is associated with a low incidence of excessive drinking (34, *pp. 45, 48, 129, 131*).

Miscellaneous Cold Beverages

During the preceding 24 hours, only 2% of the men and 1% of the women had taken a fruit drink or *limonade,* and only 1% of the men and 2% of the women had drunk fruit juice, soda or other bottled nonalcoholic beverages. Among those who drank such beverages, men on the average consumed 254 cc. of fruit drinks or limonade and 208 cc. of fruit juice or soda, and women, approximately 215 cc. of either beverage.

In these small groups of consumers, fruit drinks or limonade were taken primarily by younger respondents and by inhabitants of larger communities. Fruit juices, sodas, and especially bottled carbonated drinks, were consumed notably by younger people, the wealthy, inhabitants of large cities, and particularly by professional men, executives and college graduates.

Approximately half of these beverages were consumed at home and generally during the warm hours of the day. It should be emphasized that these results, obtained during the relatively cool time of year, cannot be taken as representative of all seasons.

The acceptance and wide use of these cold beverages—many of them promoted as suitable nonalcoholic substitutes for water—will presumably increase. At the time of this investigation they were generally available only in cities, due largely to poor distribution and the lack of refrigeration facilities elsewhere.

Coffee

The French, like many other groups, generally appreciate coffee as a stimulant and it is involved in an almost ritualistic sharing throughout the day in homes, restaurants, cafés, cantines, and even business offices. At the same time, there is a fear that the stimulation from coffee may lead to nervousness, jitteriness or insomnia. These divergent attitudes may underlie some of the reported drinking habits.

The widespread use of coffee, either black (café noir) or with milk (café au lait), is indicated in Table 5. Black coffee was taken by 67% of the men and 57% of the women at some time during the preceding 24 hours, and coffee with milk by 48% of the men and 63% of the women.

Black coffee was used by more men than women in all age, education, economic and residence groups, and in most occupations, while coffee with milk was more frequently used by women.

TABLE 5.—*Coffee Consumption in 24 Hours: Percentage of Users and Average Consumption (cc.) per User, by Population Categories*

| | BLACK COFFEE | | | | COFFEE WITH MILK | | | |
| | % of Users | | Consumption | | % of Users | | Consumption | |
	Men	Women	Men	Women	Men	Women	Men	Women
Total	67	57	223	209	48	63	316	333
Age (years)								
Under 30	71	58	227	218	50	61	329	322
30–39	70	57	247	229	49	62	301	335
40–49	70	65	231	197	50	67	320	325
50–59	70	59	195	215	42	62	326	307
60–69	55	53	198	174	48	60	304	372
70+	50	44	219	198	51	65	316	362
Occupation								
Farm owners	69	60	178	189	49	79	329	350
Farm workers	61	68	218	191	34	59	328	300
Businessmen	71	59	196	235	48	55	305	309
Professional, Executives	70		242		49		323	
White collar	70	54	217	192	52	57	288	297
Manual	72	62	255	212	46	60	315	311
Retired	48	56	200	211	56	63	323	343
Education								
Primary	66	57	228	214	48	65	321	340
Upper Primary	72	63	208	196	52	48	286	264
Technical	73	47	209	169	46	70	326	366
Secondary	74	56	221	218	52	53	304	288
College	66	61	190	161	49	45	293	257
Economic Group								
Wealthy	74	68	187	159	54	56	318	269
Well-to-do	71	61	217	209	48	62	324	335
Modest	65	56	235	217	50	61	313	339
Poor	62	51	232	208	39	69	308	331
Residence (population)								
Under 2,000	64	56	194	193	49	67	326	338
2,000–5,000	67	57	221	226	48	64	332	342
5,000–20,000	64	61	262	226	52	60	324	334
20,000–100,000	71	53	251	213	50	60	283	338
Over 100,000	70	60	216	211	42	54	307	301

In the older groups (over 59) the use of black coffee was substantially less, while the use of coffee with milk appeared more commonly. The greater use of coffee with milk in this group may be attributed in part to a greater fear of insomnia, and in part to an appreciation of the value of milk for older people.

Members of the highest economic group used black coffee more frequently than did those in the average or lower groups. This may stem from the belief among intellectuals that the stimulation of coffee will favor "brain function." Coffee with milk was used least frequently by men in the lowest group, but most frequently by women in that class.

Men who consumed these two beverages drank on the average 223 cc. of black coffee and 316 cc. of coffee with milk, while women took 209 and 333 cc., respectively. No significant quantitative differences in intake were observed in the various population categories.

The men took more than 70% of their black coffee and more than 90% of their coffee with milk at home, while the women took more than 90% of both beverages at home.

No evidence of any widespread existence of the "coffee break" was apparent. Among the French, as among other Mediterranean peoples, this phenomenon has not achieved great popularity. The men, for example, took 91% of their black coffee at breakfast, 1% at lunch and 3% at dinner, and only 4% during the afternoon. The men likewise drank 51% of their coffee with milk at breakfast, 24% at lunch and 7% at dinner; they drank 4% during the morning, 9% during the afternoon, and 4% during the evening.

Among adult Italians coffee consumption is substantially less than among the French (34, p. 50). In a typical week the average Italian who used coffee drank less than 80 cc. per day. A direct comparison between French and Italian use is impossible, however, because of the more concentrated form of coffee preferred in Italy.

Miscellaneous Hot Beverages

Various hot beverages—tea, infusions (herb teas), or chocolate—although less common than coffee, made up an important intake for many of the respondents.

Tea. As shown in Table 6, tea—traditionally a beverage of social prestige—was used primarily by women, and by those aged 40 to 70. It was taken frequently by the wives of businessmen and white-collar workers, and also by the wives of farmhands and manual workers. Use of this beverage increased markedly with education, economic status, and size of the community. Thus tea was the beverage of the well-educated, wealthy woman of the big cities.

TABLE 6.—*Miscellaneous Hot Beverages Consumption in 24 Hours: Percentage of Users, by Population Categories*

	TEA		HERB TEAS		CHOCOLATE	
	Men	*Women*	*Men*	*Women*	*Men*	*Women*
Total	3	9	6	11	3	7
Age (years)						
Under 30	2	8	1	4	7	10
30–39	2	8	2	10	2	8
40–49	2	11	8	8	3	5
50–59	4	12	8	12		7
60–69	7	11	12	21	5	6
70+	4	6	13	23	3	4
Occupation						
Farm owners	2	3	6	8	2	7
Farm workers	1	9	4	12	5	9
Businessmen	4	12	5	8	2	10
Professional, Executives	8		6		9	
White collar	5	16	6	8	4	6
Manual	1	10	5	7	3	9
Retired	8	9	14	14	4	6
Education						
Primary	1	6	6	12	2	7
Upper Primary	2	18	9	15	3	9
Technical	9	12	3	9	5	6
Secondary	8	31	7	5	7	10
College	22	45	8	3	9	6
Economic Group						
Wealthy	13	26	6	6	2	9
Well-to-do	4	9	9	12	4	6
Modest	1	9	5	10	2	8
Poor	1	3	4	14	5	8
Residence (population)						
Under 2,000	2	5	8	14	3	6
2,000–5,000	4	4	5	8	3	8
5,000–20,000	2	5	4	12	2	9
20,000–100,000	5	14	7	6	3	6
Over 100,000	5	24	4	11	5	8

The average quantity of tea consumed by actual users was 235 cc. by men and 248 cc. by women. Approximately half was taken at home with breakfast by the men, while the women drank substantial amounts during the afternoon as well as at breakfast.

Infusions. Herb teas were used even more widely—perhaps because of traditional belief in their health qualities. This may explain, at least in part, the use of infusions by older persons, retired workers, those with less education, and members of the lower economic groups.

The average quantity consumed by actual users was 183 cc. by men and 189 cc. by women, taken at meals and especially before bedtime.

Hot chocolate. This beverage, frequently awarded in Mediterranean countries to children as a prize for good behavior, was taken most frequently by the younger respondents and those with secondary-school or college education. Among actual consumers, the average quantities taken by men were 349 cc. and by women, 306 cc., for the most part with breakfast.

4. Alcoholic Beverages

The actual use of alcoholic beverages, like that of other foods, liquid or solid, represents in considerable measure the conscious or unconscious appreciation of their food, pharmacological and psychological values.

Contemporary scientific opinion regards alcohol as a food, characterized by peculiar assets and liabilities, and endowed with a particular swiftness of action. But alcohol also has effects—especially on the central nervous system—which are not usually associated with other foods.

The action of alcohol on the brain has been the subject of considerable controversy, and formerly it was hotly disputed whether alcohol is a stimulant or a depressant. It is now apparent that the psychophysiological action of alcohol, like that of other agents, cannot be described as always stimulating or always depressing. Instead, the effects depend on such factors as dosage, duration of exposure, presence or absence of other chemicals, and the particular cells or organs under consideration. Even the basis of comparison is important. Thus, what one observer may term the depressing action of alcohol on the cerebral cortex, with a resultant release of inhibitions, may be viewed by another as a stimulation—marked, for example, by heightened sexual activity.

It should be kept in mind, therefore, that the consumption of alcoholic beverages to be described herein represents efforts to achieve both physiological and psychological goals, but that the nature of these goals—and their relative importance—may not be known to the individual drinker.

Since much of this use of alcohol in France took place in cafés, it must be emphasized that these establishments are not the equivalent of the American cafe or restaurant; instead, the French café or bistrot is more like the American bar or saloon, or the British pub. The café is not only the most convenient source of alcohol away from home for both adolescents and adults but also is a center for many if not most leisure activities. This is particularly true in the lower economic groups; accordingly the French café has been aptly termed "the salon of the poor" (27, *p. 317*).

Wine (10% Alcohol by Volume)[4]

Wine, traditionally the standard beverage of France and widely regarded as healthful and nutritious, was not used by all respondents, but it was used more often than any other alcoholic beverage, and it was consumed in the largest quantities.

In the 24 hours preceding the interviews, pure wine[5] was taken by about 70% of the adults—82% of the men and 60% of the women. Among these consumers, the average intake was roughly 610 cc. by each man and 210 cc. by each woman.

It must be emphasized that these data, although secured on a statistical cross-section of the French population, indicate patterns only during the survey time and are presented entirely for purposes of comparison. They cannot be used to represent typical daily consumptions throughout the year, or to calculate total annual intake.

Approximately 30% of the adults—18% of the men and 40% of the women—either abstained completely during the day or used alcohol in a form other than wine. The actual distribution of wine consumption by various amounts is shown in Table 7, together with the percentage of all wine used in each consumption–quantity bracket.

Applying the wine-drinking pattern indicated in this survey to the French population suggests that 78% of the adults drank only

[4] Approximations of the alcohol contents, by volume, of wine, wine with water, beer, cider, aperitifs, and distilled spirits, were prepared with the kind cooperation of Mr. Sully Ledermann.

[5] A distinction is made in this report between "pure" (straight, undiluted) wine, the most commonly used form, and "wine with water" or "eau rougie," a mixture of wine with natural or mineral water which is used by many French women and children.

33% of the wine, and that 13% of them drank 51% of it. Any attempt to reduce the excessive consumption by a small fraction of the population would thus affect a considerable part of the wine economy of the country.

Table 7 shows, too, that this heavy consumption was more common among men; 2% of the men—those who drank more than 2,000 cc. a day—consumed approximately 10% of all the wine used by all men.

Among the women, 96% drank less than 500 cc. of wine in 24 hours. Scarcely 2% consumed more than 750 cc.

Comparison indicates that wine is generally used more widely but in relatively smaller amounts by Italians (34, *p.* 52). Thus, on a typical day, 30% of the French but only 17% of the Italians consumed no wine. Roughly 40% of the French men and 3% of the women, but only 15% of the Italian men and 1% of the women, drank more than 500 cc. in 24 hours.

The significance of various demographic factors is shown in Table 8.

Age. The percentage of wine consumers in the age groups 18 to 59 was remarkably constant among both men and women, with a decrease among both sexes in the oldest groups. The average intake in the period under examination was likewise constant up to age 59, with a noticeable decrease thereafter.

Sex. On the average men took three times as much wine as did women. This striking difference obviously cannot be attributed sole-

TABLE 7.—*Wine Consumption in 24 Hours, by Amounts Consumed (cc.)*

Amount Consumed	% OF SUBJECTS			% OF TOTAL WINE CONSUMED		
	Men	Women	Total	Men	Women	Total
0	18	40	29	0	0	0
10–249	21	46.5	34	7	50	15
250–499	20	10	15	15	30	18
500–749	16	2	9	18	9	16
750–999	10	1	5	17	5	15
1,000–1,499	9	0.5	5	21	4	18
1,500–1,999	4	*	2	12	2	10
2,000+	2	*	1	10	*	8
Totals	100	100	100	100	100	100

* Less than 0.5% of consumers.

TABLE 8.—*Wine Consumption in 24 Hours: Percentage of Users and Average Consumption (cc.) per User, by Population Categories*

	% OF USERS		CONSUMPTION	
	Men	Women	Men	Women
Total	82	60	610	210
Age (years)				
Under 30	83	63	649	217
30–39	83	63	748	221
40–49	86	60	670	213
50–59	85	60	702	237
60–69	75	52	434	185
70+	72	52	394	125
Occupation				
Farm owners	80	61	745	221
Farm workers	75	62	915	308
Businessmen	91	59	545	228
Professional, Executives	83		534	
White collar	86	64	497	210
Manual	85	68	724	247
Retired	72	56	378	190
Education				
Primary	81	60	635	208
Upper Primary	90	59	645	208
Technical	88	67	495	244
Secondary	84	50	520	169
College	80	61	348	177
Economic Group				
Wealthy	85	64	544	227
Well-to-do	85	67	582	205
Modest	82	58	683	206
Poor	76	58	802	206
Residence (population)				
Under 2,000	79	57	717	191
2,000–5,000	80	61	620	238
5,000–20,000	81	56	593	217
20,000–100,000	88	66	599	191
Over 100,000	87	61	635	242

ly to the greater body weight of men or their larger nutritional requirements.

Occupation. Among the occupational groups, male farm workers showed the lowest percentage of wine consumers—only 75%—but the highest individual consumption. In contrast, businessmen, professional workers, executives and white-collar workers all showed relatively high percentages of wine consumers but relatively low individual consumption. During the period of investigation the average quantity of wine drunk by farm workers was more than 1½ times that used by business officials and white-collar men.

Similar trends have been observed among Italians, who also reported the largest consumption of wine—with meals—by farmers and farmhands, and the smallest by white-collar workers and housewives (34, p. 127).

Further analysis showed that 16% of farm workers, 9% of farm owners and 8% of manual workers and domestics drank more than 1,400 cc. of wine during the 24 hours, compared with 2 to 3% of the businessmen, professionals, executives and white-collar workers. Moreover, 2% of the farm workers and 2% of the farm owners drank more than 2,000 cc., in contrast to a negligible proportion—less than 0.5%—of the upper socioeconomic groups. Since the farm workers, farm owners, manual workers and domestics represent 64% of the male population of France, these groups furnish a significant portion of the heaviest wine consumers.

It is possible that those with the highest standards of living place more emphasis on quality than on quantity. Members of the wealthy class can also turn to nonalcoholic means of relaxation: they can use synthetic tranquilizers, seek psychiatric or other medical consultation, or go to the beach or a spa.

Education. The largest percentages of wine consumers were found among those with a moderate education. But the largest consumption, especially among men, was reported by those with the least education, while college-educated men drank the smallest quantities.

Economic Groups. Improved economic status was reflected by a higher percentage of wine users among men, but a lower intake. A relatively high average consumption—about 800 cc. in 24 hours—was reported by the poorest respondents. Excessive consumption—the use of more than 2,000 cc. in 24 hours—was reported by 2% of the wealthy men, 3% of the well-to-do, 8% of those with modest income, and 9% of the poor.

It seems clear that wine can be considered the alcohol of the poor. This has been substantiated by a special study, in the city of St. Etienne, in which the wine consumption of the lowest economic class was found to be more than double that of the group of executives and professional men (4, *p. 59*).

Residence. The percentage of wine consumers was slightly less in rural localities, partly owing to substitution of other beverages in many communities. As will be shown, the use of wine was approximately the same throughout most of southern and central France, but in the northeast—in Artois, Picardy, Alsace and Moselle —it was replaced in considerable degree by beer, and in the northwest—in Normandy and Brittany—it was replaced to a great extent by cider.

Drinking With and Between Meals. The relative portion of wine consumed at different times of the day is shown in Table 9. Approximately three-fourths of the wine consumption by men and nine-tenths of that by women took place at the two main meals. Somewhat larger quantities were taken with lunch than with dinner. These data, of course, apply particularly to the autumn and winter period of the survey. It is probable that a different pattern would be noted during the hot summer months.

Women of nearly all economic and occupational groups (except farm workers) drank only 7% of their daily wine between meals. Although wine was usually readily available in their homes, they evidently did not drink during the morning or afternoon, when alcohol may be taken especially for its psychological effect. This was not true of men. Businessmen, professionals, executives and white-collar workers drank from 5 to 15% of their wine between

TABLE 9.—*Wine Consumption in 24 Hours: Percentage of Users and Percentage of Total Consumption, by Time of Day*

Time of Day	% OF USERS		% OF TOTAL CONSUMPTION	
	Men	Women	Men	Women
Breakfast	12	1	5	2
Morning	15	2	7	2
Lunch	76	54	41	52
Afternoon	21	4	10	4
Dinner	69	43	34	39
Evening	5	1	2	1
Total			99	100
Total with meals			80	93
Total between meals			19	7

meals, while farm owners, farm and manual workers and domestics took from 20 to 25% at these periods. Similarly, men of the lower economic classes drank more of their wine between meals than did those of the wealthy or well-to-do classes.

It therefore appears that those who drank the largest amounts of wine—farmers and heavy workers—did not drink much more at meals, when the food would provide a degree of protection against intoxication, but drank substantial amounts between meals.

The use of wine with or before breakfast was reported mainly in rural communities of less than 5,000 population. It is in these communities that the heaviest wine consumers—farm owners and farm workers—were also found.

Although morning drinking has been considered, particularly by some American observers, as the sign of a serious drinking problem (17, 18), there is no evidence that the relationship is universal. In many Mediterranean regions, especially in rural areas, wine and other alcoholic beverages are customarily taken with breakfast (34) without any indications of intoxication, addiction or other signs of injury.

Place of Consumption. Most wine was consumed at home. This is normal, since most French people take their meals at home, and most of the respondents drank much more wine with than between meals. Wine-drinking at the place of employment was common in men who were farm workers, farm owners and manual workers. Wine-drinking at a café or bar was reported particularly by manual and farm workers, domestics, farm owners and business proprietors.

In general, women drank little wine away from home, although female farm workers drank more than one-third of their daily wine where they worked. Of all the female groups, manual workers drank the most wine in cafés, but this consumption was small, representing only 4% of the daily intake.

Wine with Water (5% Alcohol by Volume)

Although wine with water, or eau rougie, was not drunk by a very large proportion of French adults,[6] its consumption—particular-

---

[6] In many French families it is customary for this diluted wine to be served to children. Often it is the first form of alcoholic beverage to which children are introduced. It is interesting to recall that, in earlier civilizations, drinking diluted wine was the sign of sobriety while drinking undiluted wine was viewed as intemperate.

ly by women and by older respondents of both sexes—was sufficient to warrant separate consideration. For the purpose of this report, it is estimated that the beverage is a 1:1 mixture of ordinary table wine and either natural or mineral water.

During the 24 hours preceding the interview, wine with water was consumed by 4% of the men and 9% of the women, the men drinking an average of 314 cc. (equivalent to 157 cc. of wine) and the women 242 cc. (equivalent to 121 cc. of wine). About 70% of this beverage was used by women.

The most frequent users were women aged under 30 and over 50, and men aged over 60, but in no age group did more than 13% use this beverage. Its greatest popularity was reported among retired men and women, those with moderate education, and women of the wealthy class. It was favored in smaller communities, especially in the regions of Charente, Auvergne, Limousin and Périgord. Customarily, nearly all eau rougie was taken with lunch or dinner.

Beer (4% Alcohol by Volume)

Beer is not only an important beverage in certain regions of France —especially in the northeast, near the Franco-German border—but is also popular in certain of the demographic groups. It is commonly believed to be a particularly healthful beverage, rich in carbohydrates, and especially helpful to nursing mothers, convalescent patients, and others in need of nutritive support.

During this survey, beer was used by 9% of the respondents—12% of the men and 7% of the women—in amounts averaging approximately 476 cc. by men and 270 cc. by women. Close to three-fourths of all the beer was consumed by men.

Examination of the data on specific population groups (Table 10) shows that beer was preferred primarily by the young of both sexes, by businessmen, professionals, executives, white-collar workers, manual laborers and domestics, and by inhabitants of moderate-sized and larger communities. It appeared to be particularly favored by men in the higher-educated and more economically advanced groups, though not by women in those groups. Thus beer evidently is a drink of men, of men with relatively high standards of living, and of men in big cities. It was strikingly less popular among women, among farm owners and farm workers, among those living in small communities or rural areas, and among lower income groups, who preferred wine.

TABLE 10.—*Beer Consumption in 24 Hours: Percentage of Users and Average Consumption (cc.) per User, by Population Categories*

	% OF USERS		CONSUMPTION	
	Men	Women	Men	Women
Total	12	7	476	270
Age (years)				
Under 30	16	10	592	273
30–39	14	6	476	316
40–49	12	9	478	283
50–59	12	6	347	218
60–69	5	4	363	250
70+	4	3	325	175
Occupation				
Farm owners	5	3	369	250
Farm workers	2	3	350	200
Businessmen	17	7	411	195
Professional, Executives	17		778	
White collar	13	9	265	194
Manual	18	6	559	333
Retired	3	7	500	284
Education				
Primary	11	7	474	296
Upper Primary	1	6	418	164
Technical	14	8	783	178
Secondary	18	6	281	167
College	25	°	344	°
Economic Group				
Wealthy	26	3	429	267
Well-to-do	11	6	536	258
Modest	13	9	455	274
Poor	7	3	471	390
Residence (population)				
Under 2,000	5	4	344	273
2,000–5,000	17	10	497	224
5,000–20,000	16	10	628	215
20,000–100,000	15	8	468	375
Over 100,000	16	5	400	281

° Less than 0.5% of consumers.

In part, the relative preferences for beer and wine by men with various standards of living may be due to the relative costs of the two beverages. Beer consumers were twice as numerous in the wealthy classes as in the middle income groups, and again nearly twice as numerous in the latter as in the lower income groups.

Among women, the variations between different groups were small. As with all other alcoholic beverages, the drinking patterns of women changed relatively little in the several population categories. Women of the wealthy class did not drink more beer than those in lower economic groups; on the contrary, a slightly higher proportion of consumers was reported among the well-to-do and modest income groups.

Two geographical regions were strikingly different from the rest of France. While beer was used by 12% of the men in the entire country, it was taken by 44% of the men in the north, comprising Nord, Artois and Picardy, and by 28% of the men in Alsace. Similarly, while the average beer-drinking man consumed about 500 cc. of this beverage, the comparable amounts were about 600 cc. in the north and 700 cc. in Alsace.

Among women, the proportion of beer consumers was 7% in the whole country, 32% in the north, and 19% in Alsace. In the latter two regions, the women also used beer more frequently but, unlike the men, each user did not apparently drink a larger average quantity.

More than half the total of beer consumed during the period was used at home and with the major meals. As shown in Table 11, the men consumed 63% of this beverage with meals, and only 10% in the morning, 19% in the afternoon, and 8% in the evening. All the beer consumed by women was taken with lunch or dinner.

Business proprietors were the most numerous both among those drinking beer between meals, and among those drinking it in a café.

TABLE 11.—*Beer Consumption in 24 Hours: Percentage of Users and Percentage of Total Consumption, by Time of Day*

	% OF USERS		% OF TOTAL CONSUMPTION	
Time of Day	*Men*	*Women*	*Men*	*Women*
Breakfast	*	*	3	0
Morning	2	*	10	0
Lunch	7	5	34	55
Afternoon	3	*	19	0
Dinner	5	4	26	45
Evening	2	*	8	0
Total			*100*	*100*
Total with meals			*63*	*100*
Total between meals			*37*	*0*

* Less than 1% of consumers.

Cider (4% Alcohol by Volume)

Like beer, apple cider is an important alcoholic beverage in certain regions of France—in this case, Normandy and Brittany, which produce about 95% of all the cider in the country (24).

Approximately 10% of the adult respondents—12% of the men and 8% of the women—drank cider during the 24 hours preceding the interviews. The average quantities consumed—655 cc. by men and 305 cc. by women—suggest that cider serves as a substitute for wine in many homes. It is probable that these quantities would have been even larger in the summer.

As shown in Table 12, the percentage of cider-drinking men among the various age classes was remarkably constant, ranging between 10 and 12%. The average consumption per user was likewise similar in all age groups up to 69. Among women, both the percentage of users and the average intake decreased substantially in the oldest age group.

It is apparent that cider is used largely by those who produce it. Approximately one-fourth of the rural population drank it and consumed about 53% of all the cider produced in the country. It is noteworthy that this beverage was used by 23% of the men and by 28% of the women who were farm owners, and by 29% of the men and 12% of the women farm workers. The popularity of cider among farmers explains its use by approximately 17% of all respondents in towns and villages with under 2,000 population, and by only about 3% of inhabitants of large cities.

Analysis by economic status shows that cider is essentially the beverage of low-income groups in rural areas, being used by only 9% of the men and 7% of the women in the wealthy class but by 20% of the men and 9% of the women in the lowest economic group. Among men in the latter group was found not only the largest proportion of users but also the largest average consumption per user.

Geographically, cider is used most in the areas where it is produced—notably Normandy and Brittany, and also in the center of France, including Anjou, Touraine, Berry and Orléanais. The highest percentages of cider drinkers—60% of the men and 41% of the women—were found in Normandy and Brittany, followed by Touraine and Anjou with 36% of the men and 20% of the women, and then by Berry and Orléanais with 24% of the men and 14% of the women.

TABLE 12.—*Cider Consumption in 24 Hours: Percentage of Users and Average Consumption (cc.) per User, by Population Categories*

	% OF USERS		CONSUMPTION	
	Men	Women	Men	Women
Total	12	8	655	305
Age (years)				
Under 30	12	10	638	290
30–39	11	7	700	400
40–49	12	9	758	325
50–59	14	10	711	277
60–69	10	7	688	239
70+	11	4	483	167
Occupation				
Farm owners	23	28	700	321
Farm workers	29	12	855	375
Businessmen	5	8	663	396
Professional, Executives	*		*	
White collar	7	3	511	267
Manual	9	3	600	333
Retired	9	6	432	269
Education				
Primary	14	10	668	311
Upper Primary	1	5	520	308
Technical	9	5	645	200
Secondary	4	*	500	*
College	3	3	600	300
Economic Group				
Wealthy	9	7	671	417
Well-to-do	11	7	607	247
Modest	10	8	680	276
Poor	20	9	728	374
Residence (population)				
Under 2,000	20	15	717	342
2,000–5,000	12	9	572	232
5,000–20,000	9	5	523	266
20,000–100,000	5	2	475	383
Over 100,000	4	2	727	200

* Less than 1% of consumers.

As shown in Table 13, cider—like other beverages of low alcohol content—was taken with meals by most men and by all women who drank it. Only 13% of the men drank it between meals. Cider consumed with lunch and dinner represented 80% of the total daily intake. Almost all the cider was consumed at home except by the farm workers, who drank more than half their cider away from home.

TABLE 13.—*Cider Consumption in 24 Hours: Percentage of Users and Percentage of Total Consumption, by Time of Day*

Time of Day	% OF USERS		% OF TOTAL CONSUMPTION	
	Men	Women	Men	Women
Breakfast	2	*	6	*
Morning	2	*	7	*
Lunch	11	7	44	52
Afternoon	2	*	6	*
Dinner	9	*	37	48
Evening	*	7	*	*
Total			100	100
Total with meals			87	100
Total between meals			13	0

* Less than 1% of consumers.

Aperitifs (17–20% Alcohol by Volume)

Aperitifs are characteristic beverages of France, and are used in substantial amounts by various social and economic groups. They are considered here in two categories: those based on wine and those based on other alcoholic beverages.

Wine-Based Aperitifs (17% alcohol by volume). These beverages are generally taken straight, or sec, without dilution with water. They include cocktail and dessert wines such as sherry, as well as vermouth, Dubonnet, Byrrh and Rafael. They are customarily used by men but also by a substantial number of women.

Nonwine-Based Aperitifs (20% alcohol by volume). Most nonwine-based aperitifs are based on brandy and are customarily diluted with water. They include anisette, the most widely used of this group, as well as Pernod, pastis, Ricard and Berger. Nonwine-based aperitifs were used by many men, but by so few women—less than 1%—that the consumption by women will not be dealt with.

In general, wine-based aperitifs accounted for two-thirds of all aperitif consumption during the period. It is highly probable that consumption varies considerably with season.

In some cities, as in Marseille, the use of pastis as an aperitif is so common that it must be considered a local custom (6).

Sex and Age. During the 24 hours preceding the interviews, wine-based aperitifs were used by 8% of the men, with an average intake of 136 cc., and by 3% of the women, with an average intake of 96 cc. Nonwine-based aperitifs were used by 4% of the men, with an average intake of 224 cc.

As shown in Table 14, the use of both types of aperitif was more

TABLE 14.—*Aperitif Consumption in 24 Hours: Percentage of Users and Average Consumption (cc.) per User, by Population Categories*

| | WINE-BASED | | | | NONWINE-BASED | |
| | % of Users | | Consump-tion | | % of Users | Consump-tion |
	Men	Women	Men	Women	Men	Men
Total	8	3	136	96	4	224
Age (years)						
Under 30	8	3	215	80	6	366
30–39	15	5	136	109	7	189
40–49	7	3	244	100	3	169
50–59	8	3	133	93	3	139
60–69	4	°	75	°	1	100
70+	3	°	67	°	°	°
Occupation						
Farm owners	2	°	125	°	1	100
Farm workers	°	°	°	°	2	150
Businessmen	9	6	258	106	10	341
Professional, Executives	19		140		4	75
White collar	15	°	133	83	8	315
Manual	10	8	147	113	5	172
Retired	3	1	67	77	1	100
Education						
Primary	6	2	136	109	4	193
Upper Primary	20	4	278	100	6	660
Technical	13	5	109	75	5	317
Secondary	13	3	125	83	7	125
College	19	23	175	79	5	83
Economic Group						
Wealthy	20	7	238	75	6	620
Well-to-do	8	2	186	86	4	207
Modest	8	3	136	108	4	224
Poor	4	°	107	°	4	107
Residence (population)						
Under 2,000	2	1	115	94	2	170
2,000–5,000	11	1	64	100	3	308
5,000–20,000	8	2	150	75	4	159
20,000–100,000	12	2	188	125	3	394
Over 100,000	15	8	132	95	10	204

° Less than 1% of consumers.

common among the younger groups, especially those under 40. Frequency of use as well as average amounts decreased markedly above age 60.

Occupation. Professional men and executives, white-collar and manual workers and domestics were the most frequent users of wine-based aperitifs, while businessmen and white-collar workers were the largest users of the nonwine-based aperitifs. Farmers and housewives, the retired and those without occupation rarely drank these beverages.

Education and Economic Status. No clear-cut relationship was evident between educational status and use of aperitifs, except that only a small number of users was found among those with only a primary-school education. As relatively expensive drinks, aperitifs were associated with higher standards of living. Thus, it seems that the upper classes tend to replace wine with its derivatives—either brandy or wine-based aperitifs.

Residence. Whatever their type, aperitifs were urban beverages, used much more commonly in the cities than in the country, and much more in the big towns than in the small ones.

Region. The greatest use of wine-based aperitifs occurred in the vicinity of Paris, where 27% of the men were consumers, and in Seine-et-Oise and Seine-et-Marne, 13%, in comparison with the nationwide 8%.

The highest percentage of users of nonwine-based aperitifs was found in Provence and Côte d'Azur, 13%, followed by Paris, 8%. The national percentage was 4. The average intake per user during the day was approximately 527 cc. in Provence and Côte d'Azur, 145 cc. in Paris, and 224 cc. in all of France. These are substantial quantities. For example, 527 cc. of a nonwine-based aperitif is roughly equivalent in alcohol content to a liter of wine or to five whisky highballs.

Time and Place. Both types of aperitif were commonly consumed as appetizers before lunch and before dinner, practically never before breakfast or between meals. Business owners and professional men drank an anisette, or whisky or brandy with water, usually before the evening meal. In contrast, manual and white-collar workers

—if they used such beverages at all—drank them just as often before lunch as before dinner.

About 70% of all aperitifs of both types were consumed at cafés. More than other groups, manual workers went to a café or restaurant for their wine-based aperitif, while professional men and business owners, who were among the heaviest consumers, more often drank it at home or in the homes of friends. Only about 5% of the nonwine-based aperitifs drunk by business owners was consumed in a café or restaurant, in contrast to about 60% by professional men, executives, manual and white-collar workers.

Distilled Spirits (50% Alcohol by Volume)

Distilled spirits include grape brandy (including cognac and Armagnac), apple brandy (calvados), whisky, gin, vodka, and a number of domestic and imported liqueurs. Of these beverages, grape brandy and apple brandy are by far the most common.

Although other beverages—wine, beer, cider and aperitifs—are usually served in standard container sizes for each beverage, this is not true of distilled spirits, especially when taken at home. Brandy, for example, may be taken in a liqueur glass, a cup, a wine glass, or other container. For the purposes of this report, it has been estimated that a "standard" serving of distilled spirits is equivalent to 20 cc. Undoubtedly this represents a minimum quantity, and the choice of this unit has resulted in a systematic underestimate. Furthermore, an unknown amount of brandy—unofficially estimated to be at least equal to the legal production (37, p. 46), and perhaps as much as 50% in excess (26, p. 54)—is produced illicitly on farms by home distillers, or made by the privileged bouilleurs de cru. The problem of the bouilleur de cru has long been vexing and controversial in France, and it has been repeatedly charged that these small distillers have grossly exceeded the brandy production permitted them under the tax laws. In some respects the problem is similar to that of the "moonshiner" and the manufacture of illegal whisky in the United States.

It is not known to what extent the answers of the respondents may have been colored by the illicit nature of the distilled spirits they consumed. It seems reasonable, however, to presume that the result would also be an underestimation of quantities, especially in rural areas.

It is thus necessary, in the following pages, to attach less importance to the quantities reported than to the differences which are apparent in the various consumer categories.

Users and Quantities. During the 24 hours preceding the interviews, 7% of the adults—12% of the men and 3% of the women—drank at least half a liqueur glass or 10 cc. of distilled spirits. The average quantity per user was 43 cc. by men and 30 cc. by women. Approximately 85% of all such beverages was drunk by men.

Among Italians, in a comparable survey (34, *p.* 55), about 6% of the men and 1% of the women apparently drank some distilled spirits during 1 day in the survey period.

The use of more than 30 cc. of distilled spirits in 24 hours was reported by approximately 6% of French men, compared to 1% of Italian men (34, *p.* 55). The difference between these percentages may be of particular significance.

Applying the data in Table 15 on a national scale, more than 98% of French adults drank only 41% of the distilled spirits, while less than 2% drank 43% of the total.

Less than 1% of the men consumed more than 200 cc. of distilled spirits during the 24-hour period; they accounted for 12% of all the spirits drunk by all men. These very heavy drinkers were found in roughly the same proportions in rural communities and large cities.

Further characteristics of the several population categories are presented in Table 16.

Age and Sex. The percentage of consumers in the various age groups differed little, although a slightly higher proportion of distilled-spirits consumers was found between the ages of 40 and 60.

TABLE 15.—*Distilled Spirits Consumption in 24 Hours, by Amounts Consumed (cc.)*

Amount Consumed	% OF SUBJECTS			% OF TOTAL SPIRITS CONSUMED		
	Men	Women	Total	Men	Women	Total
0	88	97	93	0	0	0
10–29	6.5	2.4	4.5	24	42	26
30–49	2	0.2	1	15	11	15
50–69	1.5	0.2	0.5	16	16	16
70–89	0.5	*	*	8	7	8
90+	1.5	0.2	1.0	37	24	35
Totals	*100*	*100*	*100*	*100*	*100*	*100*

* Less than 0.5% of consumers.

TABLE 16.—*Distilled Spirits Consumption in 24 Hours: Percentage of Users and Consumption (cc.) per User, by Population Categories*

| | % OF USERS | | CONSUMPTION | |
	Men	Women	Men	Women
Total	12	3	43	30
Age (years)				
Under 30	11	3	48	34
30–39	11	4	44	28
40–49	15	3	44	48
50–59	14	2	45	20
60–69	10	✿	34	✿
70+	12	3	39	18
Occupation				
Farm owners	18	2	41	30
Farm workers	10	✿	35	✿
Businessmen	13	3	56	22
Professional, Executives	15		74	
White collar	11	7	43	30
Manual	12	2	42	20
Retired	7	2	33	35
Education				
Primary	12	2	40	30
Upper Primary	11	4	58	26
Technical	15	3	43	30
Secondary	10	3	44	27
College	11	13	83	42
Economic Group				
Wealthy	17	3	41	33
Well-to-do	16	3	44	38
Modest	8	3	45	24
Poor	12	2	39	40
Residence (population)				
Under 2,000	14	2	40	41
2,000–5,000	12	3	58	22
5,000–20,000	10	2	56	28
20,000–100,000	12	3	43	30
Over 100,000	11	6	29	27

✿ Less than 1% of consumers.

As was generally true with other forms of alcohol, more men than women drank distilled spirits in every population category, and they drank larger amounts. In the rural groups, men outnumbered women drinkers of distilled spirits by nearly 15 to 1. The very large difference between the use of distilled spirits by men and by women may be attributed in part to the "virile" qualities popularly associated with such beverages. Because of their high alcohol content, distilled spirits have a more sudden impact on the drinker—a phenomenon which is supposed to be less attractive to women and less necessary for them. Perhaps it is because women are intrinsically better able to withstand stress, and less inclined to impulsive searches for sudden relief from intolerable situations, that their use of strong drink has been held in most cultures to be neither desirable nor ladylike.

Occupation. In two groups—farm owners and professionals–executives—the number of users was above average. Distilled spirits are thus on the one hand a cheap source of alcohol for the farmer, who very often has a private still or hires a bouilleur de cru, and on the other an expensive drink for members of the wealthier classes. In contrast, farm workers have little access to private stills, since they own neither fruit trees nor vineyards, and consumption of distilled spirits by this group is relatively low.

One group of women—office workers, especially in big cities—showed a high percentage of distilled-spirits drinkers. It is also noteworthy that wives of farmers differed from their husbands and conformed to the average behavior of all women.

Education. No relationship between educational level and use of distilled spirits was noted among men. Among women, however, the proportion of users by those with college education was markedly higher than average. In comparison with other women, these highly educated ones—working closely with men, often competing with them and tending to adopt many masculine attitudes—may be more likely to experience exceptional emotional tensions, and more prone to follow the masculine trait of seeking tranquilization in rapid-acting, high-alcohol-content distilled spirits.

Economic Status. Although distilled spirits—usually brandy purchased at a café or store—supposedly served as the "alcohol of the rich," and were used primarily by members of the upper economic groups, they were also used by substantial numbers of the poorer group. Low-cost brandies presumably offered members of the latter group an opportunity to partake of this "alcohol of the rich."

Residence. The percentage of consumers among men was much the same regardless of the size of the community in which they lived. Among women, a somewhat larger proportion was observed in the big cities, where less stigma is attached to their use of distilled spirits.

Regions. The highest percentages of consumers among men were found in Normandy, Brittany, Berry and Orléanais, where 24% of the male respondents had drunk distilled spirits—usually apple or grape brandy. Other areas with high consumption were Lyonnaise and Alpes, 15%, and Charente, Nord, Artois and Picardy, 14%. Most women users (7%) were found in Paris and in the Lyonnaise region.

Time and Place. Approximately 47% of the distilled spirits used by men and all such beverages used by women were taken with or immediately after lunch or dinner. Thus it appears that even when women tend to use a beverage preferred particularly by men, they drink it as most Frenchwomen drink all alcoholic beverages— primarily with meals. It seems probable that this characteristic has played an important role in protecting most Frenchwomen from the potential hazards of excessive drinking.

Men drank 13% of their distilled spirits between meals, during the morning or afternoon, and 22% during the evening. An additional 19% was consumed with or even before breakfast, a custom reported mostly by men in smaller communities, and by businessmen and manual workers as well as farm owners.

More than half of all distilled spirits was drunk at home, often alone, but members of the professional and executive groups drank distilled spirits mostly at cafés. One-fifth of the distilled spirits used by men and almost one-third of that used by women was consumed on Sundays.

Total Alcohol

The average ethyl alcohol content of the major French beverages, in per cent by volume, is estimated as follows: Wine, 10%; wine with water, 5%; beer, 4%; cider, 4%; wine-based aperitifs, 17%; nonwine-based aperitifs, 20%; distilled spirits, 50%.

From these values, it was determined that, with nearly three-fourths of all the French—90% of the men and 56% of the women— drinking some alcoholic beverage during the preceding 24 hours, the average consumption of absolute alcohol by the men who drank was 68 cc. and by the women who drank, 23 cc. Approximately 90%

of the alcohol consumed by both men and women was derived from wine. About 83% of the total alcohol was consumed by men.

The distribution of this consumption among population categories is shown in Table 17. It is evident that 16% of the men drank more than 110 cc. of absolute alcohol and this group consumed 42% of the total alcohol ingested by all men in the 24-hour period. Only 4% of the women drank more than 50 cc. of absolute alcohol, and they accounted for 29% of the total alcohol consumed by all women.

At the other end of the scale, 73% of the adult population—49% of the men and 96% of the women—either abstained or consumed small quantities, less than 50 cc. of absolute alcohol (equal, for example, to 500 cc. or half a bottle of wine, or to 100 cc. or 3⅓ oz. of distilled spirits).

Although 10% of the men and 44% of the women used no alcohol in any form during the 24-hour period of the survey, it cannot be assumed that they did not drink at other times.

It is interesting to note that while 28% of the French respondents abstained during the period of investigation, in a comparable study a 24-hour abstention was reported by 23% of Italian Americans and 14% of Italians (34, p. 56). At the same time it may be recalled that, in these three groups, excessive drinking has been reported to be highest among the French, moderate among the Italian Americans, and lowest among the Italians.

The characteristics of various population groups are shown in Table 18.

TABLE 17.—*Absolute Alcohol Consumption in 24 Hours, by Amounts Consumed (cc.)*

Amount Consumed	% OF SUBJECTS			% OF TOTAL ALCOHOL CONSUMED		
	Men	Women	Total	Men	Women	Total
0	10	44	28			
10–29	20	42	30	5	45	12
30–49	19	10	15	11	26	14
50–69	14	2	8	13	11	12
70–89	13	1	7	15	5	14
90–109	8	0.5	4	14	5	12
110–149	8	⎫	4	15	3	13
150–199	5	⎬	2.5	13	2	11
200–299	2	0.5	1	8	1	6
300+	1	⎭	0.5	6	2	6
Totals	*100*	*100*	*100*	*100*	*100*	*100*

TABLE 18.—*Absolute Alcohol Consumption in 24 Hours: Percentage of Users and Consumption (cc.) per User, by Population Categories*

	% OF USERS		CONSUMPTION	
	Men	Women	Men	Women
Total	90	56	68	23
Age (years)				
Under 30	95	64	72	23
30–39	94	63	77	21
40–49	96	61	69	25
50–59	93	56	71	26
60–69	80	36	44	23
70+	74	33	41	15
Occupation				
Farm owners			72	18
Farm workers			81	22
Businessmen			71	18
Professional, Executives			60	
White collar			56	18
Manual			74	21
Retired			31	14
Economic Group				
Wealthy	90	60	73	28
Well-to-do	91	58	63	21
Modest	90	55	70	23
Poor	92	51	75	22
Residence (population)				
Under 2,000	91	55	70	22
2,000–5,000	91	54	66	26
5,000–20,000	90	56	62	21
20,000–100,000	89	58	68	21
Over 100,000	93	55	69	30

Age. The percentages of consumers and amounts of absolute alcohol consumed were about the same in all age groups, both male and female, up to 60, and decreased considerably after that age. Up to 60 years, therefore, age had the lowest association with alcohol use.

Occupation. Among men, the largest quantities of alcohol were consumed by heavy laborers—farm, manual and domestic workers—followed by farm owners. Their major source of alcohol was wine. The lowest intakes were reported by professional men, executives and white-collar workers, although they drank much less wine and consumed much more aperitifs or distilled spirits, with a relatively high alcohol content. It is likely that in summer, when many heavy laborers spend more time in outdoor work, the differences between them and the other groups would be even more marked.

Among women, too, the highest consumption was reported by those who did heavy physical work—farm and manual workers and domestics.

The groups consuming the most alcohol were characterized by a relatively high intake between meals, particularly of wine, or by a significant use of brandy or other distilled spirits before or during breakfast.

Economic Groups. Apparently wine—or cider in certain areas—is the alcohol of the poor; the aperitif is the alcohol of the wealthy; and distilled spirits is the alcohol of both the wealthy and the farm owner. In large part this is a reflection of the relative cost of each beverage as a source of alcohol. The minimum prices of these beverages in cafés and stores at the time of the interviews are shown in Table 19.

It appears, however, that in whatever form, alcohol was consumed by the same proportion of users in approximately the same total quantities in each of the economic categories. The relative importance of each beverage as a source of alcohol for all men in each economic group is shown in Table 20.

TABLE 19.—*Minimum Retail Prices of Alcoholic Beverages*

Café Purchase	*French Francs*	*Equivalent U.S. Cents**	*U.S. Cents per cc. Alc.*
Wine, 100-cc. glass	20	4	0.4
Beer, 250-cc. "demi"	45	9	0.9
Wine-based aperitif, 60-cc. glass	50	10	1.0
Nonwine-based aperitif, 20-cc. glass undiluted	60	12	1.2
Distilled spirits, 20–60-cc. glass	20–200	4–41	0.4–1.4
Store Purchase (liter)			
Wine	85	17	0.2
Beer	45	9	0.2
Cider	45	9	0.2
Wine-based aperitif	600	124	0.7
Nonwine-based aperitif	1250	257	0.9
Distilled spirits	1200	248	0.6

* Comparison based on 485 "old" francs equal to $1.00.

TABLE 20.—*Relative Sources of Absolute Alcohol Obtained from Beverages by Economic Groups (Men), in Per Cent*

Beverage	Wealthy	Well-to-do	Modest	Poor
Wine	63	78	84	86
Beer	6	3	3	1
Cider	3	5	4	8
Wine-based aperitif	11	5	3	1
Nonwine-based aperitif	11	3	3	1
Distilled spirits	6	6	3	3
Total	100	100	100	100

Residence. The consumption of absolute alcohol varied relatively little by locality. In rural areas, as shown in Table 21, a lower consumption of alcohol in aperitifs was associated with a higher consumption in wine, cider or distilled spirits, depending on the region. In cities, a higher consumption of alcohol in aperitifs was associated with a lower consumption of other beverages. Women in the big cities consumed a little more absolute alcohol than did those in the smaller cities and rural communities.

Region. Among those who used alcohol in any form, the highest average quantities were consumed in Provence and Côte d'Azur (59 cc.) and in Pays de la Garonne (52 cc.); and the lowest in Normandy and Brittany (35 cc.) and Alsace (38 cc.).

Time and Place. Women generally drank all their alcoholic beverages with meals. Men, however, took about three-fourths of their alcohol with the two main meals—40% with lunch and 32% with dinner—but drank 6% with or before breakfast, 19% between meals (9% during the morning, 10% during the afternoon), and 3% in the evening.

TABLE 21.—*Relative Sources of Absolute Alcohol Obtained from Beverages by Residence Groups (Men), in Per Cent*

	RESIDENCE (POPULATION)				
Beverage	Under 2,000	2,000– 5,000	5,000– 20,000	20,000– 100,000	Over 100,000
Wine	84	76	80	79	82
Beer	1	5	7	5	4
Cider	9	5	3	2	1
Wine-based aperitif	1	5	3	6	4
Nonwine-based aperitif	1	3	2	5	6
Distilled spirits	4	6	5	3	3
Total	100	100	100	100	100

Drinking between meals was reported especially by manual and farm workers, and farm owners, who took nearly one-third of their total alcohol at such times, and also by those in the modest- or low-income groups. Farmers drank about 25% of their distilled spirits, and manual workers about 20%, before or during breakfast.

The substantial use of alcohol between meals by the French is in marked contrast to the habits of Italian adults, among whom 70% of the men drink exclusively with meals (34, *p. 71*), compared to less than 60% of French men.

Both men and women drank more alcohol on Sunday than on any other day of the week, Saturday ranking second. Almost half of all aperitifs and one-third of the distilled spirits were consumed on those two days.

Two-thirds of all the alcohol consumed by men was taken at home, 11% in cafés or bars, 7% in restaurants, 4% at the homes of friends, and 12% at places of employment or other locations. Home consumption accounted for roughly three-fourths of the wine and cider, two-thirds of the distilled spirits, and half of the beer. About three-fourths of the aperitifs, one-fourth of the beer, a sixth of the distilled spirits and a twentieth of the wine was bought in cafés or bars.

Women drank approximately 90% of their total alcohol at home and only 3% in bars or cafés.

5. Regional Alcoholism Rates

One of the striking relationships found in this survey is the variation of alcohol consumption among the different geographical regions of France. Certainly wine is not consumed uniformly by all people in all sections at all times.

1. Large numbers of Frenchmen consumed no alcoholic beverage of any kind during the survey period.

2. In substantial areas, beverages other than wine are of major importance, notably cider, apple brandy and beer. In some of these regions, the use of other alcoholic beverages exceeds that of wine.

3. Although the total amount of alcohol consumed by the average individual is not greatly affected by age—at least up to the age of 60—or by standard of living, or size of community, it is markedly affected by geographic location. This is shown in Table 22, in which the 92 departments of France are divided into the 16 major regions (see Map 1 inside front cover) as used for many economic, cultural and political surveys conducted by IFOP and other organizations.

The 16 regions are listed in order of decreasing death rates from alcoholism and cirrhosis of the liver as calculated from INSEE data (16). As Ledermann (25) and others have emphasized, the comparison of such data between countries may be difficult, but between regions within the same country it seems valid. The proportion of respondents who used each beverage during the survey period is given as the percentage of the total adult population of the region. The estimation of alcohol consumed is given as the amount of total absolute alcohol used by the average inhabitant, including drinkers and nondrinkers.

Although it is believed that the percentages of consumers of various beverages as shown in Table 22 are realistic, the amounts given as the total alcohol consumed are probably underestimated. Especially in the case of distilled spirits, such as grape brandy and

TABLE 22.—*Percentage of Users of Alcoholic Beverages, Average Absolute Alcohol Consumed (cc.) and Death Rates (per 100,000) from Alcoholism, by Region*

| | Map No. | % OF USERS | | | | | Absolute Alcohol Consumed | Alcoholism Death Rates* |
		Wine	Beer	Cider	Aperitifs	Spirits		
Normandy, Brittany	2	49	2	50	1	12	26	57
Alsace	9	66	24	1	1	4	26	48.5
Anjou, Touraine	3	60	4	28	3	7	32	45
Lyonnaise, Alpes	11	88	3	6	7	11	45	45
Nord, Artois, Picardy	1	56	38	6	5	8	30	38
Seine-et-Oise, Seine-et-Marne	16	67	10	7	11	8	33	38
Paris, Seine	15	74	12	2	21	10	40	37
Lorraine, Champagne	6	73	5	2	2	1	35	36
Burgundy, Morvan, Jura	5	82	2	5	4	4	38	32.5
Bordelais, Pays Basque	8	85	†	†	2	4	38	31
Auvergne, Limousin, Périgord	10	82	1	6	2	6	44	31
Berry, Orléanais	4	80	1	19	2	13	36	28
Charente	7	58	4	4	2	8	44	24
Pays de la Garonne	12	88	1	†	6	2	44	24
Provence, Côte d'Azur	14	76	8	†	7	4	48	24
Languedoc, Eastern Pyrenees	13	80	4	†	4	6	38	21

* National rate: 37 per 100,000.   † Less than 1%.

apple brandy, as noted above, it appears that the quantities reported by the respondents were substantially less than the amounts actually consumed. It must be emphasized again that these quantities, reported for a specific 24-hour period, cannot be used directly to indicate annual consumption; nevertheless, they are of interest for purposes of comparison.

Regional Beverage Use

Wine. The lowest percentages of wine drinkers were found in the northwest (49% in Normandy and Brittany) and the north (56% in Nord, Artois and Picardy); the highest (up to 89%) were found in the south (the Midi), where wine production is a major industry.

Beer. The highest percentages of beer drinkers were found in the north (38% in Nord, Artois and Picardy) and the northeast (24% in Alsace). The closeness of these regions to Germany, with its beer-drinking traditions, may be an important factor. Substantial use of beer was also reported in Paris and the adjacent area. In the south, however, few—8% or less—drank beer.

Cider. The highest percentages of cider drinkers were found in the northwest (50% in Normandy and Brittany), and in the center (28% in Anjou and Touraine). As with beer, cider was consumed by only a few—4% or less—of those in the south.

Aperitifs. As noted above, aperitifs appear to be a drink of the big cities. They were used by 21% of respondents in Paris and 11% in nearby Seine-et-Oise and Seine-et-Marne, but by 7% or less in other parts of France.

Distilled Spirits. These beverages were consumed by the largest percentages of respondents in the center (13% in Berry and Orléanais) and the northwest (12% in Normandy and Brittany) but by relatively few in the northeast and south.

On the basis of the survey data it appears that the total reported alcohol consumption tends to follow a geographical pattern. Thus the lowest per capita consumption—an average of 26 cc. of absolute alcohol—was noted in the northwest and the northeast, while the highest quantities—38 to 48 cc.—were reported in the south. Although no firm relationship is evident, there is a general trend toward higher consumption in the south and lower in the north.

Alcoholism Death Rates

The rates of death from alcoholism and cirrhosis of the liver in France[7] appear to be the highest in the world among reporting countries. They were 37 per 100,000 in 1959 (16). But contrary to beliefs held widely outside of France, and even accepted by many Frenchmen, the rates are by no means uniform throughout the country.

The highest reported rates, as published in 1960 (16) show 70 deaths per 100,000 in Brittany, 48.5 in Alsace, and 44.5 in Normandy. In contrast, the rates range from about 21 to 24 per 100,000 in the southern regions along the Mediterranean, and these are comparable with those in adjoining regions of Italy (25, *p. 152*).

A clear south-to-north trend of increased death rates associated with excessive drinking thus appears to characterize France. This tendency has been discussed by other workers (41; 25, *p. 141*), who have observed that it cannot be explained simply on the basis of differences in total alcohol consumption. It has also been suggested that a similar south-to-north tendency of increasing death rates from alcoholism may exist in other Northern Hemisphere countries (46). The characteristics of certain French regions—those with the highest and those with the lowest death rates—deserve further examination.

Normandy and Brittany. Reported from this region are the highest rates of death from alcoholism and cirrhosis of the liver: 82 per 100,000 in Morbihan, 76 in Côtes-du-Nord, 70 in Ille-et-Vilaine, all departments of Brittany; and 61 in Orne, 52 in Calvados, 52 in Eure, and 34 in Seine-Maritime, all departments of Normandy.

The ravages of alcohol addiction in these areas have been noted by other observers, who have described Normandy and Brittany as a "bastion of alcoholism" (25, *p. 143*). The problem of excessive drinking in one particular group—the Breton fishermen—has been so obtrusive that it has evoked a special investigation (15).

Normandy and Brittany, as noted above, had the lowest percentage of respondents who drink wine, the highest who drink cider, and one of the highest who drink distilled spirits. Yet in this region the average reported per capita consumption of total alcohol is one of the lowest in France.

[7] For convenience in expression, combined death rates from "alcoholism" and "cirrhosis of the liver" will be reported herein as rates of death from alcoholism.

Alsace. Ranking second in death rates from alcoholism, this region has departmental rates of 63 in Haut-Rhin, 47 in Bas-Rhin and 28 in Moselle.

Wine consumption in this area is relatively low, while the proportion of beer consumers is the second highest in France. Alsace ranks with Normandy and Brittany in having the lowest reported average per capita consumption of total alcohol.

Anjou and Touraine. Included here are departmental death rates from alcoholism of 62 in Mayenne, 49 in Loire-Atlantique, 49 in Sarthe, 36 in Indre-et-Loire, and 35 in Maine-et-Loire.

The proportion of wine consumers in this region is one of the lowest in France, but consumption of cider ranks second only to Normandy and Brittany, and consumption of distilled spirits—mostly apple brandy—is appreciable. The total alcohol consumption is one of the lowest in France.

Languedoc and Eastern Pyrenees. In contrast to the three regions noted above, this area has the lowest rate of deaths from alcoholism and cirrhosis of the liver. Departmental rates per 100,000 are 16 in Lozère, 20 in Aveyron, 20 in Hérault, 21 in Gard, 21 in Aude, and 26 in Pyrénées-Orientales.[8] Here wine consumption and total alcohol consumption are both high, although not the highest in France, while consumption of other alcoholic beverages is far below average.

Provence and Côte d'Azur. The death rates from alcoholism in the departments of this region are likewise low—20 in Bouches-du-Rhône, 22 in Alpes-Maritime, 23 in Hautes-Alpes, 26 in Vaucluse, 30 in Basses-Alpes, and 30 in Var.

Wine consumption is well above average, but the use of other beverages is relatively low. The average per capita intake of total alcohol is one of the highest in France.

Pays de la Garonne. This region reports the lowest rates of death from alcoholism in France: 19 in Tarn-et-Garonne, 22 in Haute-Garonne, 23 in Gers, 23 in Hautes-Pyrénées, 24 in Ariège, 26 in Tarn, and 31 in Lot.

The percentage of wine users is among the highest in France, the

---

[8] Similar rates have been reported in Piemonte, Valle d'Aosta, and Trentino-Adige in northern Italy (25).

percentage of distilled spirits users is average, and the percentage of users of cider, beer and aperitifs is below average. The average intake of total alcohol ranks as the highest of any region.

Paris. In this metropolitan area, the rate of death from alcoholism, 37 per 100,000, ranks about midway among the 16 major regions.

The use of aperitifs here is far above average, the use of cider far below, and the use of wine and distilled spirits, as well as the intake of total alcohol, are all slightly above average.

It is evident that the lowest percentages of wine users and the highest percentages of users of other beverages were found in the areas with the highest rates of death from alcoholism; and the highest percentages of wine users were in the areas with the lowest death rates. These findings, however, must be considered only with due caution. That there is no necessary correlation between alcoholism and per capita alcohol consumption has been noted by Lolli and his associates (34, *p. 3*), who pointed to the higher frequency of alcoholism in the United States—approximately eight times that in Italy—while American consumption is less than half that of the Italian.

Although in France the lowest death rates were reported in the wine-drinking areas, it is obvious that the consumption of wine cannot by itself prevent alcoholism. Nor is there any evidence to suggest that the higher death rates in regions with higher consumption of beer, cider and distilled spirits may be due to some noxious characteristic of those beverages.

It is likewise evident that during the survey period the lowest average intake of total alcohol was reported in areas with the highest death rates from alcoholism, while higher alcohol intake was reported in regions with the lowest death rates. But it would be nonsensical to infer that the reduction of alcohol intake would increase alcoholism, or vice versa.

Instead, explanations must be sought in the attitudes and actions of French alcoholics, in the attitudes and beliefs held by the normal inhabitants of the various regions, and in the personal and family patterns which govern their use of the various beverages. Ledermann (25, *p. 151*) long ago indicated the need for investigations in this complex field. These factors will be explored in the following chapters.

6. Summary

From an interview survey of all beverages consumed during a 24-hour period by a stratified sample of the adult population of France (aged over 20), the following observations, applicable to the 24-hour period, were made:

1. The average French adult drank approximately 1,000 cc. of total fluids, of which 44% was in the form of alcoholic beverages.

2. Plain or tap water was used by 34% of the respondents, bottled water by 14%, plain milk by 6%, and fruit juices, fruit drinks, sodas and other miscellaneous cold beverages by 3%. Milk was used particularly by the oldest, but hardly by young adults. Fruit juices and sodas were used primarily by the young, especially those living in big cities and with the most education and highest economic status.

3. Black coffee (café noir) was used by 62%, coffee with milk (café au lait) by 56%, infusions or herb teas by 8%, ordinary tea by 6%, and hot chocolate by 5%. Black coffee was drunk particularly by men, coffee with milk by women, herb teas—popularly assumed to have health qualities—by older women, and tea by women in the upper economic class.

4. Three out of four French adults—90% of the men and 56% of the women—drank an alcoholic beverage during the 24-hour period.

5. Wine was used by about 70% of the respondents, cider by 10%, beer by 9%, aperitifs by 8%, and distilled spirits by 7%.

6. The choice of alcoholic beverages was heavily influenced by relative cost and by geographical factors. The least expensive source of alcohol was wine, followed in order by cider, beer, distilled spirits and aperitifs.

7. Wine was used most commonly in the south or Midi. The lowest percentage of consumers but the highest per capita intake was found among farmers and manual workers, while the highest percentage of users but the lowest individual intake was found among those with the highest occupational levels and standards of living.

8. Beer tended to replace wine in such northeastern regions as Nord, Artois, Picardy and Alsace. Throughout France, it was used especially by well-to-do men in the larger cities.

9. Cider tended to replace wine in the northwest, notably in Normandy and Brittany, where it was used by half the respondents, more particularly by farm workers and other low-income groups.

10. As relatively expensive beverages, aperitifs were consumed primarily by younger men with high occupational and economic status, and most widely in Paris, Provence and Côte d'Azur.

11. Distilled spirits—including grape brandy, apple brandy (calvados), whisky, gin, vodka and liqueurs—were used particularly by three groups:

farm owners, especially those with private stills and exercising the privileges of the bouilleur de cru or home distiller; men of the wealthy class in the larger cities; and women with the highest education. The largest numbers of consumers were in Normandy, Brittany, Berry and Orléanais.

12. Nearly all alcoholic beverages taken by women were consumed with lunch or dinner. Men, however, drank approximately one-fifth of their cider, one-fourth of their wine, one-third of their beer, one-half of their distilled spirits, and nearly all of their aperitifs apart from food. Drinking between meals, whatever the beverage, was especially common among male farm workers, farm owners, manual workers and the lower income groups.

13. Approximately 13% of the adults drank 51% of all the wine. Approximately 16% of farm workers, 9% of farm owners and 8% of manual workers drank more than 1,400 cc. of wine during the 24-hour period, compared with between 2 and 3% of businessmen, executives, and professional and white-collar workers. The consumption of more than 2,000 cc. was reported by 2% of the wealthy men, 3% of the well-to-do, 8% of the modest, and 9% of the poor. Those who drank the largest amounts of wine did not drink much more than others at meals but drank substantial amounts between meals.

14. Less than 2% of the respondents drank 43% of all the distilled spirits; less than 1% of the men accounted for 12% of all distilled spirits used by all men.

15. About 16% of the men drank 42% of the total absolute alcohol consumed by all men, and 14% of the women drank 55% of all the alcohol used by all women. The number of men who used alcohol in any form was not affected substantially by age up to 60, economic status, occupation or size of community. Among women, the number of users decreased steadily with age, but increased with economic status.

16. The amounts of alcohol consumed by men were not affected substantially by age up to 60 or size of community, but were related to economic status and occupation. The largest quantities were used by farm workers and manual laborers, and by the poor. Among women, the largest amounts were used by the wealthy and those living in large cities.

17. The lowest percentages of wine users and the highest percentages of users of other beverages were found in the areas with the highest death rates from alcoholism and liver cirrhosis, notably Normandy and Brittany in the northwest. The highest percentage of wine users was found in the areas with the lowest death rates from alcoholism and cirrhosis, notably Languedoc and Eastern Pyrenees in the south. Thus no direct relationship was apparent between total absolute alcohol consumption and the prevalence of alcoholism as suggested by these rates in the various regions of France.

18. A comparison of the drinking of the French and Italian populations shows the following: *(a)* The average total fluid consumption in a 24-hour period, both alcoholic and nonalcoholic, by the French was about 1,000 cc., and by the Italians, 900 cc. *(b)* Drinking exclusively with meals was reported by nearly 60% of the French men and nearly 95% of the French women, and by 70% of the Italian men and 94% of the Italian women. *(c)* The proportions of consumers of milk, fruit juices, sodas, beer and aperitifs were about the same in both groups. *(d)* Wine was used by 70% of the French and 83% of the Italians. *(e)* More than 500 cc. of wine was consumed in 24 hours by about 41% of the French men and 3% of the French women, and by 15% of the Italian men and 1% of the Italian women. *(f)* Distilled spirits were used by 12% of the French men and 3% of the French women, and by 6% of the Italian men and 1% of the Italian women. *(g)* More than 30 cc. of distilled spirits was consumed in 24 hours by about 6% of the French men and 1% of the Italian men. *(h)* Total abstention from alcohol during the 24-hour period was reported by 27% of the French and 14% of the Italians.

Chapter 2

POPULAR ATTITUDES TOWARD ALCOHOL

1. Introduction

IN SHAPING the behavior of the individual, it is evident that not only the immediate family but society itself plays an effective role. An example of social influence is the changed attitude toward smoking by women during the past half century, a change possibly not unrelated to an increased incidence of lung cancer in women. New social attitudes have also led to a decrease in obesity, especially among young women—this goal long urged by physicians but which apparently could not be achieved directly by health education.

In the case of alcohol use, it seems possible to visualize processes of "social engineering" (42) which could modify undesirable drinking habits by first affecting undesirable relevant attitudes. With such a possibility in mind, it becomes important to recognize that the quantitative consumption of alcohol represents only one phase of man's ability to use alcoholic beverages either wisely or unwisely. Equally important are the attitudes toward drinking.

In France, the people have long maintained a strong and colorful tradition in which alcoholic beverages—and wine in particular—have occupied an honored position in history, drama, poetry, art and economics. Wine has been almost universally regarded as the national drink, responsible for some of the particular virtues of the French. It has been said that "Without wine, France would probably not be France. The wine and the vine are not only a material heritage for France. They are also something constituting the grandeur of our tradition" (37, p. 80). Pasteur's dictum, "Wine is the most hygienic of all beverages," has survived almost as a national motto in France, although it has been attacked in the French Academy of Medicine (37, p. 82).

The wide acceptance of wine has also been accompanied by an equally wide toleration of copious drinking. "There exists in France," one observer has stated (41, p. 129), "a tender indulgence for the joyous and glowing drunkard, a genuine admiration for the man who can handle wine well." Malignac and Colin (37, p. 60) have noted

48

that "In a number of social groups, drinking is the same as affirming one's personality. In these circles, the first glass—like the first cigarette—well before and perhaps even better than the first feminine conquest—signifies in the eyes of the adolescent, initiation to manhood. The widespread expressions like 'drinking like a grown-up,' or 'drinking like a man,' are of such a nature as to make the adolescent who does not drink have a real inferiority complex. One can go even so far as to judge the value of a man by the amount of alcohol he can drink without manifesting intoxication, and to organize drinking competitions."

The popular social acceptance of intoxication in France may be indicated by the many synonyms for inebriation in the French language. These include the following: *gazé* (gassed), *gris* (gray), *noir* (black), *blindé* (armor-plated), *cuite* (cooked), *gelé* (frozen), *dans le brouillard* (in the fog), *sous la table* (under the table), *teinté* (tinted), *mûr* (ripe), *poivré* (peppered), *rétamé* (from tin-plated), *brindezingué* (from zinc-plated), *dans les vignes du Seigneur* (in the vines of the Lord), *ébrèché* (chipped), *saoul comme un Polonais* (drunk as a Pole), *en plein cirage* (fully waxed), *parti* (gone), *être rond* (to be round), *avoir du vent dans les voiles* (to have the wind in the sails), *avoir un coup de trop* (to have one blow too many), *avoir un coup dans l'aile* (to have one in the wing), *avoir un verre dans le nez* (to have a glass in the nose), *avoir sa culotte* (to have one's breeches), *plein comme une bourrique* (full as a donkey), *allumé* (lit), *biberonné* (from nursing bottle), *ému* (stirred), *se piquer le nez* (to pickle one's nose), *entre deux vins* (between two wines), *un pilier de cabaret* (a pillar of the saloon), and *se salir le nez* (to dirty one's nose).

In this respect, the French appear to be much like many Americans who, likewise, consider intoxication socially acceptable and likewise have a rich vocabulary to describe it. In contrast, however, there is a paucity of such terms in the language of the Jews and the Italians, who do not accept intoxication as a comical condition.

In the belief that alcohol consumption is strongly influenced by public opinion, the French government established the High Committee for Study and Information on Alcoholism in 1954. Among its major objectives were the measurement of French public opinion on alcohol and the modification of its attitudes in the direction of moderation.

In 1948, even before the High Committee was conceived, one

public opinion poll served to indicate some French attitudes toward alcohol and alcoholism shortly after World War II (5). A second survey (2) in 1953 gave evidence of some changes in process.

METHOD OF SURVEY

The present investigation was based on a series of interviews conducted by trained personnel with 2,726 men and women throughout France during the period from 2 to 19 September 1955. The respondents were selected on the basis of the 1954 census to give a stratified sample of the adult population of the country. Although the major purpose was to determine what the French people think about alcoholism, its extent, causes, and possible remedies, their statements likewise reveal their attitudes at the time toward the nature of alcoholic beverages and how these beverages may be used safely.

Description of Sample

Although the 2,726 respondents in the present survey were different from the 3,005 men and women whose 24-hour beverage consumption was described in Chapter I, the two groups are closely comparable in distribution by sex, educational level, economic status, region, and type of residence. For reasons not related to the present inquiry, however—largely to permit comparisons with earlier opinion polls—the present sample was divided differently into age and occupational groups.

Age. The respondents were grouped as follows: 20–34 years, 35%; 35–49, 30%; 50–64, 22%; 65 or older, 13%.

Occupation. By occupation of the head of the family, the sample was divided as follows: farmers (including farm owners and workers), 26%; business and professional men, 15%; white collar workers, 21%; manual workers, 27%; retired or no occupation, 11%.

2. VALUATION OF ALCOHOLIC BEVERAGES

Most Frenchmen are convinced that alcoholic beverages—especially wine—are beneficial. Two-thirds of the respondents endorsed the view that wine is nourishing, strengthening, and necessary to complete a good lunch or dinner.

As shown in Table 23, however, quite different qualities were attributed to other beverages. Aperitifs were considered valuable primarily because they contributed to cheerfulness and social ease, facilitating human relationships, while distilled spirits were believed to provide warmth and to go well after a meal. Oddly, aperitifs were believed to be relatively unimportant in stimulating appetite or aiding digestion.

TABLE 23.—*Qualities Attributed to Wine, Aperitifs and Distilled Spirits by Respondents, in Per Cent*

Quality	Wine	Aperitifs	Spirits
Nourishing	65	4	3
Gives lift, strengthens	66	9	17
Warming	47	11	58
Aids digestion	17	5	51
Stimulates appetite	0	2	0
Completes a good meal	66	16	55
Cheers, makes happy	55	35	34
Aids human relationships	34	24	16
None	3	40	15

A definite change in some of these attitudes—perhaps reflecting in part the recent activities of government and health agencies—was observed in comparison with earlier years. For example, the statement that wine is nourishing was approved by 79% in 1948, by 70% in 1953, and by 65% in 1955. The same view was expressed by approximately 79% of respondents in Italy in 1954 (*34, p. 122*).

The high popular regard for wine in France was likewise demonstrated by the belief of 58% that wine is useful for men engaged in heavy labor; an additional 28% thought it indispensable for such workers. The youngest respondents were less inclined to pronounce wine indispensable, but its usefulness was approved almost equally by all respondents. Only 10% considered wine useless and 2% declared it harmful. But while most agreed that wine is necessary for heavy laborers in France, 63% of them inconsistently affirmed that nonwine-drinking workmen in foreign countries are not inferior to Frenchmen. Only 28% felt that wine is indispensable or useful for athletes, while 56% held it useless or even harmful.

Here, too, changes in attitudes were apparent. The value of wine for laborers was affirmed by 95% in 1948, 88% in 1953, and 86% in 1955; its value for athletes was endorsed by 35% in 1948, 27% in 1953, and 28% in 1955.

As might be expected, the value of wine in heavy work was supported most enthusiastically by the heavy workers themselves: 89% of manual workers and 90% of farmers approved wine as indispensable or useful, in contrast to 82% of white-collar workers and 83% of businessmen and professionals. Similarly, the danger of wine for athletes was endorsed by approximately 70% of white-collar workers but only by about half of the farmers and manual workers.

Popular Safe Limits

The inquiry on the value of wine was supplemented by questions on the maximum daily amounts which respondents thought heavy laborers, office workers, women, and children under the age of 10, could safely drink. As will be noted later, these estimates are intimately involved with the widely prevalent view that a relatively definite threshold exists for alcoholism, and that there is little risk of addiction if this threshold is not passed.

Table 24 shows the generality of the view that a manual worker can drink twice as much as an office worker; a woman, two-thirds as much as an office worker; and a child, one-third as much as a woman.

That a woman should drink less than a man, even if she holds the same job, was generally accepted.

For heavy laborers, the average approved safe limit was 1,800 cc. of wine daily; but 29% of the men and 40% of the women set the limit

TABLE 24.—*Estimations of Maximum Safe Amounts (cc.) of Daily Wine Ingestion for Selected Users, by Population Categories*

Group	Heavy Workers	Office Workers	Women	Children under 10
Total	1,800	830	550	170
Sex				
Men	1,950	850	600	200
Women	1,650	800	500	150
Age (years)				
20–34	1,700	800	500	150
35–49	1,800	850	550	150
50–64	1,950	900	600	200
65+	1,800	850	550	200
Occupation				
Farmers	2,000	950	600	200
Business, Professional, Executives	1,700	750	500	150
White collar	1,600	750	500	150
Manual	1,900	850	550	150
Retired	1,700	800	500	150
Education				
Primary	1,950	900	600	200
Upper Primary	1,600	750	450	150
Technical	1,700	750	500	150
Secondary	1,600	750	500	150
College	1,450	700	500	100

at 1,000 cc., while 17% of the men and 10% of the women put it at 3,000 to 4,000 cc., and 6% of the men and 3% of the women at 4,000 cc. or more. It may be noted that 4,000 cc. of wine is equivalent in alcohol content to about a liter of brandy or whisky.

For office workers, 33% of the men and 40% of the women set the safe limit at 500 cc. of wine, while 5% of the men and 2% of the women put it at 2,000 cc. or more.

For children, 2% of the men and 1% of the women felt the limit could be set safely at 750 to 1,000 cc. but 33% of the men and 42% of the women preferred that no wine be used.

For all users, lower limits were usually recommended by those in the lower age groups, by those in the white-collar and executive occupations, and by those with the most education.

It is interesting that, in the mind of the public, the safe daily limit for heavy laborers was an average of approximately 1700 cc. of wine in 1948, 1600 cc. in 1953, and 1800 cc. in 1955. In a comparable survey in 1954, Italians held that heavy workers could safely drink 1400 cc. of wine per day (34, *p. 131*).

Dangers in Beverages

Opinions were elicited also on the possible inherent danger of certain beverages even if used in moderation. As shown in Table 25, distilled spirits and aperitifs were most frequently considered to be dangerous—more often by women than by men—while wine and beer were viewed as the safest alcoholic beverages. Interestingly, wine was considered dangerous by 7% of the respondents while coffee was so labeled by 20%, water by 2% and milk by 2%.

The possible dangers in even moderate quantities of distilled

TABLE 25.—*Beverages Considered Dangerous by Respondents, in Per Cent**

Beverages	Men	Women	Total
Distilled spirits	50	65	57
Aperitifs	40	54	47
Coffee	18	22	20
Wine	4	9	7
Beer	4	7	5
Water	3	2	2
Milk	2	2	2
Fruit juice	2	1	1
None	38	25	32

* Totals more than 100% because of multiple answers.

spirits and aperitifs were mentioned least often by farmers and manual workers, but most frequently by businessmen, white-collar workers, and professionals.

Drinking with Meals

From tradition, personal experience or medical advice, most adults were convinced that it is healthier to take alcohol when there is food in the stomach. About 80% felt it is better to drink with meals, 2% said it is better to drink between meals, 13% thought one time was as good as another, and 5% offered no opinion.

These attitudes parallel the views on the relative safety of the various types of beverages, since wine, beer and cider are commonly taken with meals, aperitifs and distilled spirits more often between meals. It is noteworthy that the safety of drinking with meals was affirmed by an almost identical number (79%) of Italians (34, *p. 131*). But while the overwhelming majority of Italians apparently put their beliefs into practice, drinking almost exclusively at meal-times, this was not true of the French. Whereas the average Italian rarely eats without drinking or drinks without eating, the French frequently separate the two functions. As noted in Chapter I, drinking between meals accounted for a substantial portion of the alcohol intake of the French, particularly by farmers and manual workers, and more especially in the consumption of distilled spirits.

Alcohol vs. No Alcohol

In northern Europe and America some groups reject the use of alcohol in any form or amount on moral or religious grounds. This attitude is seldom encountered in southern European countries.

When the French respondents were asked to give their opinion on the over-all value of wine and other alcoholic beverages taken regularly and in moderation, approximately 38% agreed that such use had a good influence on health and character, 43% said it had no particular effect, and 13% thought it had a bad influence.

When asked, "What do you think of people who drink only water and nonalcoholic beverages?" approximately 28% gave their approval, with such comments as these:

"I admire and envy them."
"They are none the worse for it, and even better off."
"They are healthy, well-balanced people."

Another 32% gave neutral answers:

"They are probably on a diet."
"They do it for health reasons."
"It is a question of taste or habit."
"They have a right to do it."
"It is probably for economy, or because of poverty."

Another 26% expressed disapproval:

"Their position is extreme."
"They are biased."
"They are snobs."
"They would be better off to drink some."
"They don't know how to live."
"They deprive themselves of what is good, and are to be pitied."
"They are weak, less vigorous, more susceptible to disease."
"They are people who are sad."
"They are not very sociable."

The attitudes on abstaining were clearly influenced by age and occupation; it was approved by about 27% of those in the middle age groups and by 30 to 33% of those in the youngest and oldest groups, 22% of farmers, 28% of manual workers, 30% of businessmen and professionals, and 34% of white-collar workers and the retired.

3. THE NATURE OF ALCOHOLISM

Perhaps the most illuminating opinions expressed by this representative sample of the adult French population are those which concern their definitions of alcoholism and their understanding of the extent of alcoholism in their country. Many of the misconceptions and misunderstandings which have created confusion both in and outside of France may stem from these attitudes.

The Definition of an Alcoholic

In most countries, there has been a growing acceptance of the concept of the alcoholic as one who has a strong urge to drink, who can stop drinking only with great difficulty, and whose drinking has created serious personal or social problems (21). Furthermore, physicians and laymen alike, especially in northern Europe and the United States, increasingly appreciate the emotional factors underlying excessive drinking and realize that an alcoholic cannot revert to moderate drinking but must abstain completely and permanently from all alcoholic beverages.[1]

These concepts, however, apparently are not widely accepted in France. Although some French writers have noted the addictive drinking of alcoholics and the antisocial aspects of their alcohol consumption (25, *pp. 107-109*), these phases are not generally considered. The overwhelming majority of French physicians and laymen believe that an alcoholic can drink moderately "if he really wants to." In addition the overwhelming majority of the respondents in this investigation defined the alcoholic mainly on the basis of when he drinks, or what he drinks, or how much he drinks.

Thus, for 90% of the respondents an alcoholic is a man who drinks at a café or bar several times a day; for 70% he is a man who drinks a glass of brandy or wine each morning at breakfast; for 50% he is a man who drinks a liter or more of wine at each meal; for 37% he is a man who drinks an aperitif before each meal; and for 14% he is a man who is intoxicated several times a year.[2]

Respondents aged 20 to 49 were least likely to associate alcoholism with occasional intoxication, but were most inclined to define it on the basis of frequent visits to a bar. On the other hand, those aged over 65 were most likely to view occasional intoxication as alcohol addiction. Those aged between 20 and 34 were most inclined to consider the consumption of a liter of wine at each meal, or drinking at breakfast, as marks of addiction.

Among occupational groups, manual workers were the least likely to define alcoholism on the basis of aperitif use before each meal, and farmers were least likely to base their definition on drinking brandy or wine with breakfast, or using a liter of wine at each meal. Retired people least frequently associated alcoholism with drinking at a bar or café several times a day. All of the opinions seemed to reflect the personal habits of the members of each group.

Excessive Drinking

Although the French had been exposed for many years to strong statements, by both medical and governmental authorities, characterizing their use of alcohol as excessive, a substantial portion of

---

[1] Some recently reported exceptions (8) are not thought to impair the general validity of this rule.

[2] The total is more than 100% because of multiple responses.

the people remain unconvinced. Approximately 60% of the respondents—54% of the men and 66% of the women—agreed that there is excessive drinking in France, but 32% to 39% of the men and 25% of the women denied the existence of such excesses, and 8% had no opinion.

By age groups, 65% of those between 20 and 34, 60% of those between 35 and 49, and 55% of those over 50, agreed that the French drink too much. It appears, thus, that the problem is perceived more clearly by the younger men and women.

The prevalence of excessive drinking was likewise recognized by 53% of those with only a primary school education, 71% of those who had attended upper primary school, 63% of those who had attended technical school, 74% of those with a secondary school education, and 81% of those who had attended a college or university.

There was division also by occupation, excessive drinking being recognized by 45 to 55% of farmers and heavy laborers, 59% of the retired, and 70 to 75% of white-collar workers and executives. At the same time, approximately two-thirds of the respondents thought that heavy laborers drink too much, one-third thought that office workers and children drink too much, and one-fourth believed that women drink too much. However, 37% felt that the average Frenchman drinks no more than the average American, 30% that he drinks no more than the average Italian, and 24% that he drinks no more than the average Englishman. In general, Americans were reputed to drink more than Italians and the English, and Italians were considered to have about the same intake as the French.

These beliefs contradict the realities: the average adult intake is 30.0 liters of absolute alcohol per year in France, 14.2 in Italy, 8.8 in the United States, and 8.5 in Great Britain (25, p. 68). In addition, the foregoing attitudes indicate not only a highly biased view of alcoholism in the United States—presumably due to widely publicized cocktail parties, drunken driving accidents, and Skid Row districts—but also a comforting rationalization among Frenchmen that their excessive drinking is no worse than that in other countries.

Alcoholism in France

Although the rates of alcoholism vary drastically among the regions of France, this fact was not known to about half the respondents; 48% stated that addiction was about equally common throughout the country. Others, however, evidenced considerable awareness of regional variations. About 30% named the distilled-spirits-producing areas of Normandy, Charente and the west as having the highest rates of alcoholism, 15% named Brittany, 8% pointed to the wine-producing areas of Burgundy and the Gironde, and 4% named the Midi. About 20% listed industrial and mining centers, generally in the north, and 5% named Paris.

The better educated the respondent and the higher his occupational status the more likely he was to recognize Normandy and Brittany as areas with high alcoholism rates. The better educated were also more inclined to name industrial centers as heavily affected by alcohol addiction. Interestingly, the inhabitants of the wine-producing regions rarely considered that alcoholism was common in their areas, but inhabitants of Normandy and Brittany most often cited their own region.

More than 40% of the respondents believed that all occupational groups were about equally affected by alcoholism. Of those with specific opinions, 44% named "laborers, manual workers and miners," 10% "the wealthy," 8% "farmers," 7% "the poor," 2% "officials," and 1% "sailors."

Regardless of the respondents' own education or occupation, most of those who had an opinion agreed that the problem was particularly acute among manual laborers. Those with the highest education exhibited an appreciation of the fact that the problem is also serious among farm owners.

Results of Alcoholism

Although the survey indicated that a large segment of the population was unaware of the extent of the problem of alcoholism, or of the regions and occupational groups which might be particularly involved, the responses indicated that the public had become aware of at least some of the dangers of alcohol addiction. Thus 88% said they had been told that alcoholism contributes to serious illness; 74% specifically cited liver ailments and 61% mental disease. About 90% agreed that alcoholism "always" or "fairly often" leads to physical deterioration, change of character, decreased occupational capability, waste of resources, and family problems. While 80% felt that alcoholism "always" or "fairly often" has a hereditary influence on children, only 60% thought that this constitutes a serious handicap for such children.

On the other hand, almost half of the respondents estimated the role of alcohol in causing industrial accidents as infinitesimal or nonexistent. Manual workers most frequently expressed this opinion. But about three-fourths of the subjects estimated that alcohol was responsible for at least one-third of all automobile accidents.

Although detailed statistical evidence is not available, it has been estimated that at least 20% of the industrial accidents and nearly three-fourths of the automobile accidents in France are attributable to excessive drinking (25, *pp. 187, 216; 37, p. 37*).

In general, as Stoetzel (49, *p. 71*) has observed, the respondents attached most importance to the effects of alcoholism on health, the troubles it causes in family life, and the hereditary consequences. Even though public health authorities had emphasized the costs of hospital and psychiatric care of alcoholics, this factor was little appreciated.

Causes of Inebriety

Although it has been widely assumed by foreigners that excessive drinking, intoxication and alcoholism in France are all due to over-indulgence in wine, this is not the belief of the French people themselves. In the present survey, 51% named distilled spirits as the beverage primarily responsible for intoxication, 44% named aperitifs, 27% named wine, and 2% named beer, cider or other beverages.[3]

In the areas where distilled spirits are produced, especially in the west, distilled beverages were cited by 57% of the respondents. In the wine-producing areas—as in the Midi—wine was named by only 18%.

Questions about basic reasons for excessive drinking evoked a multitude of answers. Thus 24% stated that too many occupations lead to drink, another 24% blamed the easy availability of many alcoholic beverages, 20% put the responsibility on such factors as "personal misery" and "poor housing," 6% suggested that France produces too much wine and other alcoholic beverages, and 3% mentioned such reasons as "habit," "natural tendency," or "the French like to drink." The two major groups of reasons—on the one hand, easy availability and excessive advertising, and on the other, misery, poor housing and occupational factors—were cited by about the same numbers of respondents.

[3] Multiple choices account for a total over 100%.

The tendency of substantial numbers to blame such factors as "personal misery" and "poor housing" as the causes of excessive drinking is not peculiar to the French. The same attitude was observed recently in Poland (3). However, Chinese, southern Italians, Jews—including the Jews in Poland—and American "dust bowl migrants" of the early 1930's all underwent misery, poor housing and squalor without any significant increase in excessive drinking.

In the present study, manual workers and farmers most frequently insisted that their occupation was responsible for excessive drinking. Farm owners—least affected by the housing situation in France—least often blamed poor housing.

The better educated respondents showed more awareness of the emotional factors involved in alcoholism and were more likely to cite personal problems and less likely to blame occupational factors.

Further questions to determine whether the respondents considered alcoholism the result of environment or of personal factors revealed that 31% believed alcoholism to be entirely the fault of the victim, 51% considered it the consequence of environment, and 4% thought both responsible. The older were more likely to blame the victim himself. The younger and the better educated were more likely to blame environmental factors alone, or both personal and environmental factors.

Control of Alcoholism

Nearly all respondents agreed that a fight against alcoholism was important—"very important," 68% and "fairly important," 25%—but the success of any such campaign was seriously doubted, especially by those in the lower economic groups. The chances of reducing the number of alcoholics were regarded as good by 81% of the wealthy, 72% of the well-to-do, 69% of those in modest circumstances and 58% of the poor.

There was likewise a marked difference in attitudes toward the various methods which had been proposed to combat alcohol addiction. A list of these methods, together with the attitudes of the men and women who were interviewed, is presented in Table 26. Almost every method was favored more by women than by men. The more specific the measure and the more it threatened to affect personal habits and interests, the less approval it received. Thus the education of youth was almost unanimously endorsed but the limitation of alcoholic beverages was viewed negatively.

TABLE 26.—*Respondents' Attitudes on Proposed Antialcoholism Measures, in Per Cent*

Measure	Men In Favor	Women In Favor	Total In Favor
Educate youth	91	93	92
Educate public	86	73	80
Severely punish intoxicated delinquents or known alcoholics	71	84	78
Reduce output of alcoholic beverages	68	78	73
Decrease number of sales outlets	63	79	71
Encourage manufacture and consumption of nonalcoholic beverages	63	73	68
Suppress alcoholic beverage advertising and publicity	63	69	66
Suppress privilege of private stills	52	53	52
Increase taxes on alcohol	39	53	46

Opposition to some measures varied with occupation. For example, reducing the number of sales outlets was denounced by manual workers, business executives and professional men, who frequent such outlets during the business day, but was not opposed by retired people. On the other hand, the suppression of private stills was acceptable to most people except the farmers who use them. In opposing higher taxes on alcohol, all occupational groups were in strong agreement.

The better educated gave more support to reducing the number of outlets, lessening the production of alcoholic beverages, suppressing the privilege of private stills, and raising the taxes on alcohol. These more highly educated individuals showed the least enthusiasm for punishing intoxicated delinquents or known alcoholics, or for suppressing advertising or publicity favorable to alcoholic beverages. Reduced production of wine was favored by 32% of all respondents, but 49% were opposed and 19% were uncertain. In contrast, 64% favored reducing the production of distilled spirits, 18% were opposed, and 18% had no opinion.

Most strongly opposed to any decrease in wine production were inhabitants of the wine-producing regions. But it was in the regions of distilled spirits production, surprisingly, that the largest percentage—70% of respondents—approved a decrease in spirits output.

A comparison of the present opinions with those expressed in the 1953 survey reveals some striking changes. For example, reducing the number of sales outlets was approved by only 26% in 1953 but by 71% in 1955. In 1953 only about 10% had favored increased taxes on alcohol, severe punishment for intoxicated delinquents, and limitation of the production of distilled spirits; in 1955 these measures were approved by roughly half of the respondents.

Of particular interest are the opinions expressed on suppressing the activity of the bouilleurs de cru, the small local distillers who are thought grossly to exceed the legal limits on their production. In the present survey, 52% favored rigorous control of the bouilleurs de cru. A later survey, conducted by IFOP early in 1960, revealed that approximately 50% of all French adults favored abolishing the tax privilege of the home distillers, 30% favored continuing the privilege, and 20% were neutral (14). Those who favored control of the home distillers attacked the practice on the grounds that it increased alcoholism, led to abuses, and was marked by fraud. In July 1960 the Government enacted legislation which protects the present home distillers in their privileges for their lifetime, and allows their bequeathal only to spouses, but forbids the issuance of new privileges.

Drinking and Attitudes toward Alcoholism

Although no effort was made in this survey to obtain quantitative estimates of alcohol intake, the respondents were asked how often they drank wine, whether or not they liked distilled spirits or aperitifs, and how often they drank at a café or bar. On the basis of their answers, the respondents were divided into 10 classes, ranging from highest to lowest consumers, and the attitudes of these classes toward excessive drinking were compared. The composition of the groups gives support to findings reported in Chapter 1.

Prominent among the heaviest drinkers were men between the ages of 50 and 65, heavy laborers, and men with relatively little schooling. Throughout, men drank progressively less as their level of education was higher. Among women, the heavier drinkers were in the younger age groups, the manual and white-collar workers, wives of such workers, and businesswomen. Women with a moderate education drank less than those with very little or very high education. In this study too, above-average consumption was reported in the below-average alcoholism region of the wine-producing Midi.

Table 27 shows the opinions expressed by four of the consumption classes, Nos. 1, 4, 7 and 10. Class 1, the heaviest drinkers, is composed of those who drink wine with lunch and dinner, like

TABLE 27.—*Opinions Expressed by Selected Consumption Classes on Problems of Alcohol, in Per Cent*

	Highest Class 1	Moderate Consumers Class 4	Moderate Consumers Class 7	Lowest Class 10
Definition of alcoholic (men)				
Several times daily to café	64	90	98	94
Brandy or wine at breakfast	46	67	90	82
Liter of wine at each meal	28	45	67	68
Aperitif before each meal	13	37	52	60
Intoxicated several times yearly	6	10	15	16
Is there excessive drinking in France?				
Yes	40	58	75	74
No	53	32	21	18
No answer	7	10	4	8
Value of wine for heavy laborer				
Indispensable	63	31	19	15
Useful	33	61	67	46
Useless	1	5	12	19
Harmful	0	1	0	12
No answer	3	2	2	8
Nondrinking foreign laborers				
Inferior	34	12	6	3
Not inferior	47	61	73	65
No answer	19	27	21	32
Value of wine for athlete				
Indispensable	12	3	1	0
Useful	40	30	16	14
Useless	17	29	35	19
Harmful	17	25	34	45
No answer	14	13	14	22

distilled spirits or aperitifs, and drink at a café at least once a day. Class 4, moderate drinkers, includes those who drink wine with lunch and dinner, and like distilled spirits or aperitifs, but never or only rarely drink at a café. Class 7, more moderate drinkers, consists of those who drink wine with only one meal a day, like distilled spirits or aperitifs, and go to a café not more than a few times each month. Class 10, the lightest drinkers, comprises those who practically never drink, like neither distilled spirits nor aperitifs, and never or rarely drink at a café; it includes also those who abstain for medical, moral or other reasons.

Unquestionably, the opinions of these respondents were closely related to their personal drinking customs. While heavy drinkers took a relatively tolerant view of frequent drinking at a bar, drinking before breakfast, drinking an aperitif before each meal, and a liter of wine with each meal, these practices were considered by many moderate drinkers as signs of alcoholism. Occasional intoxication was said to be definitive of alcohol addiction by 6% of the heaviest drinkers, 10 to 15% of the moderate and 16% of the lightest consumers. Similarly, the lightest consumers felt most strongly that there is too much drinking in France, that water-drinking workers are not inferior to the wine-drinking ones, and that wine is useless or harmful for athletes and those doing heavy labor.

These opinions were supported by the maximum limits set by each group for the amount of wine which could be safely ingested daily by heavy laborers and white-collar workers. These limits were put at 2,550 and 1,000 cc., respectively, by respondents in Class 1, at 1,950 and 850 cc. by those in Class 4, at 1,450 and 700 cc. by those in Class 7, and at 1,250 and 600 cc. by those in Class 10.

Similar trends appeared in the opinions of the various groups on the value of decreased alcohol production. Nevertheless, even among the heavy drinkers (Class 1) 10% favored reducing wine production and 27% favored reducing the production of distilled spirits. At the other extreme, among the lightest consumers and abstainers (Class 10) 20% opposed reducing wine production and 8% opposed reducing the production of spirits.

4. SUMMARY

In an interview survey of a stratified sample of the French population aged over 20, conducted in 1955, attitudes toward alcohol were elicited.

1. Two-thirds of the respondents believed that wine is nourishing and strengthening, three-fourths that it is useful or indispensable for heavy laborers, and one-fourth that it is useful or indispensable for athletes. These favorable attitudes, however, had declined somewhat since 1948. Four-fifths of the subjects stated it was healthier to drink only with meals, but a substantial portion of the alcohol intake occurs between meals.

2. The average recommended "safe limit" was thought to be 1,800 cc. of wine daily for heavy laborers, 830 cc. for office workers, 550 cc. for women, and 170 cc. for children aged under 10. Higher limits were set by heavy laborers and by respondents with the least education.

3. Distilled spirits were considered to be unhealthy or dangerous beverages by 57%, aperitifs by 47%, coffee by 20%, wine by 7%, beer by 5%, water by 2%, milk by 2%, and fruit juices by 1%.

4. Widespread tolerance of alcohol intoxication was expressed as was the view that heavy drinking is a mark of virility.

5. An alcoholic was defined by 90% of the respondents as a man who drinks at a café or bar several times a day; by 70% as a man who drinks with breakfast; by 50% as one who drinks more than 1,000 cc. of wine at each meal; by 37% as one who drinks an aperitif before each meal; and by 14% as a man who is intoxicated several times a year. Approximately two-thirds agreed that there is excessive drinking in France, but this was denied by one-third. Two-thirds asserted that heavy laborers drink too much, one-third thought that office workers and children do, and one-fourth that women do.

6. Half of the respondents were unaware of the particular gravity of alcoholism in certain vocational groups and geographical areas. Nearly 90% were aware that alcoholism contributes to serious illness, but only 50% recognized the role played by excessive drinking in automobile and industrial accidents.

7. The beverage most often involved in excessive drinking was considered to be distilled spirits by 51%, aperitifs by 44% and wine by 27%. Excessive drinking was blamed by 24% on the ready availability of alcohol, by 24% on the requirements of certain occupations, and by 20% on "poor housing" and similar personal problems.

8. As measures to combat alcoholism, education of youth was approved by 92%, punishment of alcoholics by 78%, reduced production of alcoholic beverages by 73%, reducing the number of sales outlets by 71%, increased production of nonalcoholic beverages by 68%, suppression of alcoholic-beverage advertising by 66%, suppression of private stills by 52%, and increased taxes on alcohol by 46%. Reduced production of wine was approved by 32% and opposed by 49%, while reduced production of distilled spirits was approved by 64% and opposed by 18%. Except for education of the young, all proposed control measures were approved by more women than men, and approval of all the proposals had increased significantly over recent years.

9. Attitudes were closely related to personal drinking habits, with the lightest consumers most inclined to claim that the French drink too much, to view daily café visits or drinking with breakfast as a sign of alcoholism, to question the usefulness of wine, to set lower "safe limits" for daily wine consumption, and to approve decreased production of wine and distilled spirits. Even these light consumers, however, took a relatively tolerant view of occasional intoxication.

10. Possibly presaging an eventual change in French public opinion, it was the youngest adults who most clearly recognized the prevalence of excessive drinking, were most aware of the uncontrollable nature of drinking by alcoholics, recognized the gravity of the problem of alcoholism in Normandy and Brittany, recommended lower safe limits for daily wine consumption, and approved reduced production of alcoholic

beverages, limiting the number of outlets, suppressing private stills, and increasing taxes on alcohol. These young adults were less inclined to claim that wine is "indispensable" for heavy laborers, but agreed with those in older age groups that it is "useful."

11. A comparison of the attitudes of the French with those of a parallel Italian sample showed the following: (a) The nourishing and strengthening qualities of wine were endorsed by 65% of the French and 79% of the Italians. (b) Essentially the same proportions—80% of the French and 79% of the Italians—emphasized the safety of drinking only with meals. (c) The safe limit of wine which could be drunk daily by a heavy laborer was put at about 1,800 cc. by the French and at 1,400 cc. by the Italians. (d) Toleration or social acceptance of intoxication was common among the French but rare among the Italians.

Chapter 3

MEDICAL ATTITUDES TOWARD ALCOHOL

1. Introduction

DURING THE MANY DECADES in which the problem of alcoholism has been the center of a major controversy in France, French physicians have played an important role, presenting ostensibly authoritative views on whether or not the problem exists, its seriousness, its causes, and its possible control. But these views—in the press, on the radio, in professional meetings, and in legislative hearings—have been marred by disagreement.

Divergences in medical opinions are not restricted to France, nor are they limited to alcoholism. In this case, however, the conflicting opinions and testimonials have confused both the public and government officials, not to mention observers in other countries.

One possible explanation of disparate medical attitudes toward alcohol may be fundamental differences in training and outlook between southern European physicians on the one hand, and northern European and American doctors on the other.

In England and the United States, for example, the healing arts are not the exclusive domain of the physician. It is understood that the biochemist and the bacteriologist, the psychologist, the social worker, the sociologist, and other paramedical or nonmedical specialists contribute significantly to medical research and to the prevention and treatment of disease. One result, especially in recent decades, has been an expanded awareness of the psychosomatic and psychosocial aspects of disease.

In contrast, in such countries as Italy and France, essentially all activities in the healing arts are dominated by physicians. With rare exceptions, the potential contributions of the psychologist, the social worker and the sociologist are not readily recognized. The result has been an overemphasis on the strictly somatic implications of disease.

Whether or not one system is necessarily better than the other, it is evident that the two are different.

The attitudes of the French physicians, to be detailed below, show these differences in training and focus, with their major emphasis on the strictly somatic factors involved in the uses and abuses of alcohol.

The fact that it was considered advisable to interview a substantial number of gastroenterologists gives added point to these statements. These specialists were selected because of the widespread belief—among both physicians and patients—that such complaints as indigestion, gastric distress, and a syndrome rather vaguely described as "liver disease," are the chief clinical conditions involved in excessive drinking and alcoholism, and are the conditions which most urgently require medical treatment. Gastroenterologists are the specialists most often engaged to provide that treatment. It is true, of course, that abuse of alcoholic beverages over a prolonged period may cause organic disorders of the gastroenteric tract. It is also true, however, that many diseases of the digestive system have a predominantly or exclusively emotional cause, and in the case of excessive drinkers, this is especially likely. The revealing opinions of this group of French medical men will thus serve to indicate some of the bases for popular misunderstandings on the problem of alcohol, as well as for some of the divergent views on etiology, therapy, and prevention.

METHOD OF SURVEY

Between 23 November and 9 December 1959 trained personnel interviewed a total of 200 physicians, of whom 190 are classified as *practicing physicians* and 10 as *alcoholism experts.*

Although it is believed that the opinions expressed by these respondents are generally representative of the attitudes held by most of their colleagues, the sample is not so constructed that it can be taken as formally representative of the entire French medical profession.

Description of Sample

Practicing Physicians. Included among the 190 respondents grouped as practicing physicians were 20 neuropsychiatrists, 17 gastroenterologists, and 153 family doctors. Of the family doctors, 48 were selected from the Paris area, 30 from the distilled-spirits-producing northwest of France, notably Normandy and Brittany, 29 from the wine-growing south or Midi, and 46 from other sections of the country. The three categories—neuropsychiatrists, gastroenterologists and family doctors—are believed to be those most frequently concerned in the routine observation and clinical treatment of alcoholics.

Approximately 2% of these physicians were under 30 years of age, 34% between 30 and 39, 33% between 40 and 49, 23% between 50 and 64, and 8% 65 or older. Nearly 90% were engaged primarily in private practice and most of their patients were of average or modest economic status.

Alcoholism Experts. The 10 physicians classified as alcoholism specialists were chosen from among the most highly regarded research workers in the field. They included 3 directors of neuropsychiatric centers specializing in the observation and treatment of alcoholics; 3 directors or chiefs of service in psychiatric hospitals; the director of a national institute for research on public health problems; an alcoholism expert attached to the World Health Organization; an investigator attached to a national institute for sociological research; and the head of a center for research and prevention of alcoholism.

2. VALUATION OF ALCOHOLIC BEVERAGES

Although it is customary in France—as in the United States and other countries—to assume the existence of a standard or almost universal "medical opinion" on such matters as alcoholic beverages and alcohol addiction, the opinions of the French physicians were sharply divided, frequently contradictory or inconsistent, at times exhibiting unawareness or disregard of objective research data. Some opinions seemed to be related to the medical specialty of the individual; others appear to reflect the physicians' geographic location.

It appears, therefore, that the views of some physicians are not more objective or scientific than those of the general public. This situation, of course, is not unique to the profession in France.

Practicing Physicians

Although the usefulness of alcohol as a source of energy has been established by controlled research, and the caloric value of alcohol has been ascertained by many workers (1, 7, 11, 36, 38, 39, 43), half of the practicing physicians were either unaware of these findings or disputed them. Thus, 49% stated that alcohol is a source of energy but 48% said that it has no such value.

Wine. About half of the practicing physicians accepted the traditional prestige of wine and described it as a valuable energy-yielding food, or as a tonic or stimulant, while about 40% claimed that it has no value, and about 10% termed it harmful. Interestingly, none of the doctors practicing in the wine-producing Midi considered wine to be a deleterious beverage.

In contrast to the family doctors, the neuropsychiatrists and the gastroenterologists were less willing to accept the beneficial qualities of wine.

The views of these physicians on the value of wine for men doing heavy physical labor are shown in Table 28. As noted in Chapter 2, 58% of the French public considered wine to be useful for manual laborers and 28% thought it indispensable, but these views were shared by only 45% and 5%, respectively, of the doctors.

While wine was highly regarded, at least by half of the practicing physicians, it was considered by equal numbers to be a principal factor in the alcoholism of urban labor groups, and to have a predominant role in rural alcoholism. Few physicians, however, thought wine to have a deleterious influence in the well-to-do class, and whether its consumption by alcoholics was considered a cause or a result of alcoholism was not clear.

While about three-fourths of the family doctors in Paris, the west and the miscellaneous areas of France, and one-third of the neuropsychiatrists and the gastroenterologists, believed that the use of wine by alcoholics is increasing, three-fourths of the family doctors in the Midi and nearly half of the specialists stated that it is either decreasing or constant.

Beer was thought to be unchanged or increasing in importance as a cause of intoxication, but again there was a wide divergence in views. This beverage was only rarely considered primarily responsible for alcohol intoxication in either rural or urban areas, or among those with a high standard of living.

Cider was infrequently mentioned as an important factor in the drinking of alcoholics. Even in the west, where cider production and use is greatest, its role in the alcoholism of the rural population was mentioned by only about 10% of the physicians. In the opinion of most doctors—especially those in the west—cider had lost much of its popularity in recent years.

TABLE 28.—*Views of Neuropsychiatrists, Gastroenterologists and Family Doctors on Value of Wine for Manual Laborers*

	Neuro-psychi-atrists	Gastro-enterol-ogists	FAMILY DOCTORS				
			Midi	*West*	*Paris*	*Other*	*Total*
Indispensable	0	0	3	0	2	4	9
Useful	5	8	15	13	22	22	85
Useless	11	5	9	15	17	17	74
Harmful	4	4	0	2	5	2	17
No answer	0	0	2	0	2	1	5
Total	*20*	*17*	*29*	*30*	*48*	*46*	*190*

Aperitifs, especially such nonwine-based drinks as Pernod and pastis, were believed to be significantly involved in excessive drinking only among the well-to-do. Both family doctors and specialists rated aperitifs ahead of wine and second only to distilled spirits as the intoxicating beverage of those with the highest standard of living. But in rural areas, even in the Midi, where aperitifs are relatively common, their consumption was considered of minor importance as a cause of intoxication. Practitioners in the Midi and the west, however, believed aperitifs were gaining in importance as a cause of intoxication, with inhabitants of the Midi following their traditional taste for anisette or nonwine-based aperitifs and those of the west preferring varieties based on wine.

Distilled Spirits. The majority of doctors reported that distilled spirits—mostly brandy and liqueurs—constituted the major beverages of wealthy alcoholics, rivaled only by similarly expensive aperitifs. These high-alcohol-content beverages were infrequently linked to the excessive drinking of the labor class, but one-third of the physicians cited them among the major factors in rural alcoholism. Physicians in the west frequently stressed the importance of the brandy produced by the bouilleurs de cru in the excessive drinking in Normandy and Brittany.

In general, a majority of the physicians thought that distilled spirits were losing their popularity except in the areas with the highest rates of alcoholism and particularly in the west, where these beverages maintained their traditional prestige as local products.

This divergence in medical opinions has been reported previously. Thus in 1950, Perrin found that 470 of 721 physicians considered wine the primary cause of alcoholism in France, 140 blamed aperitifs, and 111 blamed distilled spirits (41, *p. 136*).

Safe Limits

Although most of the doctors did not consider wine harmful, the daily limits they set for consumption were noticeably lower than those proposed by the French public (Chapter 2).

Whereas the public proposed a maximum of 1,800 cc. of wine daily for heavy laborers, the practicing physicians recommended 900 to 950 cc. For office workers the respective limits set were 830 and 530 cc.; for women, 550 and 360 cc.; and for children under the age of 10, 170 and 30 cc.

Family doctors in the Midi recommended somewhat higher limits than did those in other parts of the country. Differences between the recommendations of neuropsychiatrists, gastroenterologists and family doctors were usually slight, but for young children the family doctors usually approved a maximum of 30 to 50 cc. of wine a day and the neuropsychiatrists only 10 cc., while the gastroenterologists recommended none at all.

The recommendation of individual physicians covered a wide range, as in Perrin's 1950 survey (41, *p. 137*), when 1% recommended complete abstinence for heavy laborers, 68% set their limit at a liter, 8% set it lower and 24% higher.

Alcoholism Experts

The experts in alcoholism did not differ radically from the practicing physicians in their general attitudes toward alcoholic beverages, except by somewhat less approval of all forms of alcohol, but in their ideas of safe limits they differed decidedly. Although some suggested limits ranging from 1,000 to 2,500 cc. of wine a day, most indicated that the manner of drinking was far more significant than the amount.

One stated: "A quantitative threshold for excessive drinking cannot be determined because the variation in individual tolerance is too great." Most of them agreed that a "safe limit" for any occupational, age or sex group would be unrealistic because of the individual variations in tolerance, experience and nutritional status. At the same time, most of them opposed the popular view which attributes a greater capacity for alcohol to the heavy laborer.

3. The Nature of Alcoholism

The diversity of attitude among medical men on the nature of alcohol addiction was even more striking than their lack of agreement on the nature of alcoholic beverages.

Definition of an Alcoholic

Practicing Physicians

Approximately three-fourths of the physicians thought of alcoholism as related simply and clearly to the regular consumption of alcohol beyond a certain limit. Thus 29% defined alcoholism primarily as excessive use. Typical statements were: "The alcoholic is a man who uses an excess of alcohol of all kinds"; "Alcoholism is too great an absorption of alcohol in all forms"; "Alcoholism is too much alcohol in the blood"; "Alcoholism is excessive consumption, regardless of states of intoxication."

Another 29% defined alcoholism in terms of habitual or regular consumption: "An alcoholic is a man who drinks too much regularly"; "Alcoholism is regular absorption of alcohol, even at a low rate"; "Alcoholism is daily and prolonged impregnation with alcohol"; or "The alcoholic is one who drinks chronically."

Another 15% defined alcoholism in terms of consumption beyond individual tolerance: "The alcoholic is a man who drinks beyond his own capacity"; "The alcoholic drinks more than he can eliminate, and the excess of alcohol passes into his blood"; "Alcoholism is consumption in amounts higher than those which can be assimilated by the organism."

In contrast, only about 14% of the practicing physicians suggested a definition which took cognizance of psychological factors: "The alcoholic is one who loses control of his consumption and cannot limit himself"; "An alcoholic is an intoxicated man who needs to drink"; "The man who succumbs to drinking is one who is already deeply upset"; "The alcoholic is one who looks to intoxication for help in personal difficulties."

It was the neuropsychiatrists who more often emphasized an emotional imbalance existing even before alcoholism became clinically recognizable. In contrast, almost all of the gastroenterologists emphasized excessive intake, and most declared that the toxicity of alcohol manifests itself mechanically, purely on the basis of quantities consumed, and independently of individual characteristics.

The opinions of the family doctors were usually closer to those of the gastroenterologists than to those of the neuropsychiatrists. Most of them defined alcoholism in terms of excessive intake of alcohol—particularly as regular, habitual excessive drinking. Only one family doctor in seven even made mention of a compulsion to drink or any other psychological factor. These attitudes were similar to those of the public, which placed major emphasis entirely on the amount and frequency of alcohol consumed.

Alcoholism Experts

Nearly all of the 10 experts considered alcoholism inextricably related to mental problems. The significance of psychological factors was indicated by quoting such a statement as "alcoholism is the loss of freedom to abstain from alcohol" (25, *p. 119*). Most of the experts agreed that alcoholism is both an intoxication, with symptoms and sequels, and a pathological state characterized by a compulsion and a weakening of the will. But two declared that the role of alcohol is more important than that of the drinker. "Alcoholism," one of these stated, "is a combination of excessive consumption of alcohol plus a dietary deficiency."

Alcoholism in France

Practicing Physicians

The great majority of the doctors believed that the drinking habits of the French constitute a health risk for the population, and at least half described the risk as very serious.

This opinion was held by nearly all of the neuropsychiatrists and gastroenterologists. Among the family doctors, however, those practicing in the viticultural Midi appeared to consider the problem as less serious, and one-third of them stated that it was of relatively minor importance.

Whatever their location or type of practice, almost all of the physicians stated that alcoholism affects different social groups in different degrees. Manual workers were thought to be the most heavily affected by 78% of the doctors, heavy laborers by 29%, shopkeepers, salesmen, brokers, deliverymen and café owners by 29%, farm owners by 28%, the well-to-do by 28%, the "poor" by 12%, and farm workers by 3%.

Although detailed statistics are not available, there are indications that alcoholism is in fact highly prevalent among farm workers, with high rates also among fishermen and manual laborers.

Ledermann's statistical studies (25) have shown that the death rates from alcoholism, cirrhosis of the liver and "liver disease" rose steadily until the beginning of World War II, dropped spectacularly from 1942 to a minimum in 1945–1946, and then began to rise steadily, exceeding the prewar maximum by 1954–1955. The opinions expressed by the doctors on this subject were remarkably diverse. One-third of the practicing physicians said that alcoholism was increasing and one-third that it was decreasing. An increase was seen mostly by the gastroenterologists, a decrease mostly by the family doctors.

The diverging opinions on trends in the incidence of alcoholism appeared to be due to different perspectives. Most of the doctors who reported that alcoholism was increasing based their judgment either on personal experience in practice or on current statistics. Those who thought that alcoholism was decreasing usually based their opinions on observations of what they described as more sober habits of young people.

The observation of a growing sobriety among young French people was reported by nearly one-third of the doctors. But the factors to which this change might be related were not clarified.

Alcoholism Experts

Seven of the experts asserted that alcoholism was declining in France, due largely to the campaign against alcohol and the growing use of nonalcoholic beverages. All agreed, nevertheless, that the decrease was small and that alcoholism remained one of the three or four major health hazards.

The experts disagreed sharply on the seriousness or even the existence of what had been termed an "epidemic" of alcoholism among children. Most concurred that some children sometimes drink to excess, and may occasionally become intoxicated, but doubted that there was much addiction to alcohol among children.

Two of the experts denounced what they termed the "alcoholic myth," and stated that the label of alcoholic had been frequently but erroneously applied to many individuals who consumed relatively large quantities of alcohol and were occasionally intoxicated but showed no signs of addictive drinking, or were suffering from other diseases of uncertain diagnosis.

Causes of Alcoholism

Practicing Physicians

Although most of the doctors ignored emotional or psychological aspects in their definitions of alcoholism, these aspects were more often taken into account when the causes of alcoholism were considered.

Most of the factors proposed as "most decisive" in leading to alcoholism represented individual traits of the alcoholic: character weaknesses, lack of education, constitutional abnormalities, a search for escape or oblivion, a craving for alcohol. "Excessive drinking is more a consequence than a cause," one physician stated. "At the origin, there is a physical or emotional deficiency which creates a need for alcohol through the creation of a habit."

Less frequently cited were psychosociological factors involving both the individual and his environment: the influence of vocational and living conditions, poor organization of leisure time, the attractions of cafés and bars, alcoholic beverage advertising, various biases and prejudices, and the traditional indulgence of the French in drinking. One physician said, "The French are too accustomed to settle their affairs in the café, and to end their chance meetings there." Another said, "Too many people are poorly housed. They seek escape in cafés, where they get used to drinking." And another said: "It's the pull of the environment—one feels he is a man who knows how to drink."

Finally, some doctors noted such socioeconomic factors as the miserable housing and working conditions of the lower economic groups, as well as the low cost of alcoholic beverages and their virtually unrestricted production and sale. "It is too easy to get alcohol; there are no beverages to take their place at the same price."

Some of the practicing physicians indicated that alcoholism is usually due to the combined influence of multiple and varied factors. These more sophisticated views were more common among the family doctors in the Paris area and among the neuropsychiatrists.

By and large the neuropsychiatrists placed most weight on individual factors, and specifically on such psychological characteristics as individual disposition and the need for evasion, escape and compensation. In contrast, the family doctors—especially those in Paris—found major significance in the effect of living conditions, housing and the standard of living. In the areas with the highest alcoholism rates, however, family doctors seemed more inclined to place major blame on individual and psychosocial factors.

There was a tendency to attribute importance to different causative factors in different segments of the population. Thus in the working class, alcoholism was most often attributed to difficult living and working conditions, poor housing, low standards of living, inadequate diets, fatigue, heat, and the influence of excessive drinking by fellow workers. In rural areas, the contributory factors were seen as poor diet, custom, and the effect of uncontrolled spirits production and the influence of the bouilleurs de cru. In the well-to-do class, blame was placed on fashionable drinking at social affairs, social acceptance of heavy drinking, and excessive consumption in the business world. For alcoholism among business and sales people the doctors blamed general business customs, especially the tradition of settling matters in a café.

Most of the practicing physicians indicated that certain factors commonly blamed for alcoholism were having an increasingly harmful effect in France. The most important of these were held to be the living conditions of the population dwelling in slum areas and the effects of alcoholic beverage advertising. But it was also suggested that other forces were tending to limit the development of alcoholism by reducing drinking, including recent increases in the price of alcoholic beverages, public education on alcohol, improvement of living conditions for certain groups, and the development of leisure activities and sports participation especially for young people.

Alcoholism Experts

Only a few of the experts presented such extreme views as "alcoholism is caused solely by a prealcoholic personality," or "alcoholism is determined by economic, social, regional, vocational and even national factors." Instead, most of these men agreed that both internal and external factors are intimately involved.

One expert said that an "alcoholic heredity" plays an important role. All the others pronounced this view illusory.

The experts thought that various etiological factors may lead to different forms of alcoholism. One, for instance, pointed to different forms of alcoholism noted in different occupational categories. Several experts mentioned the possibility that different causative factors could be responsible for the cyclic or episodic pattern of drinking observed in British and American alcoholics, and the chronic drinking noted in French alcoholics.

Control of Alcoholism

Practicing Physicians

Approximately 31% of the physicians favored measures to reduce the production of alcoholic beverages as a means of curtailing excessive drinking; 17% urged intensified education of youth, 16% urged intensified education for young and old alike, 15% proposed more concrete and dramatic information on the effects of alcoholism, 9% thought that underlying social problems should be solved first, and 4% called for control and limitation of alcohol sales.

The family doctors generally described the current antialcoholism campaign as ineffectual. They considered it to be monopolized by the great specialists on alcoholism, and insufficiently outspoken. They complained that the entire medical profession had not been adequately consulted and properly associated in the program.

Alcoholism Experts

Most of the experts stated that they had only limited practical experience in the antialcoholism campaign, and a very modest part in its direction. They were unwilling to assess proposed control measures except to urge increased research.

Treatment of Alcoholics

Practicing Physicians

Nearly 50% of the physicians stated that psychotherapy in some form is essential for the treatment of an alcoholic patient. Somewhat inconsistently, however, only 11% of them—15% of the neuro-psychiatrists, 23% of the gastroenterologists, and 9% of the family doctors—said they would actually prescribe such care as a part of long-range follow-up therapy.

Alcoholism Experts

The experts were in agreement that psychotherapy and general medical care were both essential in immediate as well as long-range treatment, and all would prescribe this broad form of therapy. They suggested, too, that effective treatment must provide both individual and family psychotherapy.

4. SUMMARY

Opinions of 190 practicing physicians and 10 medical alcoholism experts in France were elicited by trained interviewers.

1. While 49% of the practicing physicians were aware that alcohol can serve as a source of nutritive energy, 48% denied this. Similarly, equal numbers of these doctors considered wine useful or indispensable for heavy laborers and useless or harmful. Half of the doctors considered excessive wine drinking a principal factor in the alcoholism of urban labor groups and of all rural groups, but there was no agreement on whether this use of wine represented a cause or a symptom of alcoholism. Neither beer nor cider was believed to play an important role in excessive drinking. Aperitifs and distilled spirits were believed to be involved in the

excessive drinking of the well-to-do. One-third of the doctors thought distilled spirits played a particularly important role in rural alcoholism.

2. Maximum safe limits for daily consumption of wine were set by the practicing physicians at 950 cc. for a heavy laborer, 530 cc. for an office worker, 360 cc. for a woman, and 30 cc. for a child. The alcoholism experts generally declined to set limits, believing that the manner of drinking was more significant than the quantity. Most of the practicing physicians considered habits of alcohol consumption in France to represent a major health hazard. Nearly one-third reported observing the development of more moderate drinking habits and increased sobriety among young men and young women.

3. Three-fourths of the practicing physicians defined an alcoholic essentially in terms of excessive or regular consumption of alcohol. Most of the alcoholism experts defined alcoholism in terms of emotional problems and addictive drinking. Several of the alcoholism experts noted that the label "alcoholic" was frequently erroneously applied to individuals who showed no signs of addictive drinking but merely exceeded some arbitrary quantity of intake.

4. The practicing physicians considered the most decisive factors in the origin of alcoholism to be such individual traits as character weakness, lack of education, constitutional abnormalities, a search for escape or oblivion, or a craving for alcohol. Less frequently cited were psycho-sociological factors such as poor vocational and living conditions, poor organization of leisure time, the attraction of cafés, the effect of alcoholic beverage advertising, and "tradition." Also mentioned were such socio-economic factors as poor housing, poor working conditions, the low cost of alcoholic beverages, and the virtually unrestricted production and sale of such beverages. The alcoholism experts considered a combination of personal and environmental factors to be always involved.

5. For the control of excessive drinking, reduction in alcoholic beverage production was approved by 31%, education of youth by 17%, more dramatic antialcohol propaganda by 15%, and limitation of alcoholic beverage sales by 4%. Approximately 10% thought that underlying social problems should be solved first.

6. Half of the practicing physicians stated that psychotherapy was needed for the treatment of an alcoholic patient but only 10% would actually prescribe such therapy. All of the alcoholism experts felt that psychotherapy was essential, and all would prescribe it.

Chapter 4

GENERAL DRINKING PATTERNS

1. INTRODUCTION

THE DRINKING HABITS of French adults and their attitudes toward alcoholic beverages have presumably evolved from their early drinking patterns—especially from the nature of their introduction to alcohol during childhood and adolescence, and from the attitudes of their own parents. These factors were found to play a major role in the behavior and attitudes of both moderate and excessive drinkers in Italy and other countries (9, 29, 31, 40, 44, 51).

To obtain some insight into French drinking patterns and to examine the forces possibly involved in their origin, a separate survey was conducted in a group of 2,035 men and women selected to comprise a statistically representative sample of the adult French population. This group, interviewed between 20 July and 3 August 1959, was different from both the group studied to determine consumption habits (Chapter 1) and the group studied for the analysis of attitudes (Chapter 2). Nevertheless, as each group is representative of the French population, the data from the separate studies are comparable.

METHOD OF SURVEY

For the purposes of this study, France was divided into five major regions—Paris and Seine; the Northwest; the Northeast; the Southwest; and the Southeast (see Map 2 inside back cover). In each area, the respondents were selected according to the proportional sampling method ("quota-sampling") so that the group thus obtained represented a model of the population according to sex, age, occupation of head of family, and residence.

From each respondent the interviewers obtained as much as possible of the desired information on his (or her) drinking practices during his own childhood, adolescence and adult life. It is emphasized that the data here refer to the childhood and adolescence of the adults interviewed during the survey; they do not pertain to those who are children or adolescents in France today.

Also included in this survey were questions on present alcohol consumption, making it possible to divide the group into moderate and heavy drinkers.

Description of Sample

Sex. The 2,035 respondents consisted of 51% men and 49% women.

Age. The respondents were divided as follows: 20–34 years, 32%: 35–49, 24%: 50–64, 28%; 65 and over, 16%.

Marital Status. Approximately 14% were single, 73% married (12% without children, 61% with children), 10% widowed, and 0.5% divorced. Marital status was not ascertained in 2%.

Region. Seventeen percent were from Paris and Seine, 20% from the Northwest, 25% from the Northeast, 15% from the Southwest, and 23% from the Southeast.

Education. Sixty-four percent had completed primary school (6 years); 16%, upper primary (8 years); 8%, technical (8 years); 10%, secondary (12 years); and 2%, college.

Occupation. Twenty-two percent were farm owners or workers; 9%, businessmen; 4%, professionals and executives; 17%, white collar workers; 33%, manual workers; 15%, housewives or retired.

Residence. By size of the community in which they lived, the respondents were divided as follows: less than 2,000 population, 36%; 2,000–5,000, 13%; 5,000–20,000, 17%; 20,000–100,000, 14%; more than 100,000, 20%.

2. CHILDHOOD AND ADOLESCENT PATTERNS

Earliest Drinking Experiences

Approximately four-fifths of the subjects were able to recall some details of their initial experience with alcoholic beverages. In a survey of Italians, similarly, 82% could recall their first exposure to alcohol (34, *p. 63*).

As shown in Table 29, 25% of the French respondents had tasted some alcoholic drink by the age of 6, 41% by the age of 9, and 61% by the age of 12. There were substantial differences by sex.

The average age at first drink was 9.7 years (boys, 9.3, girls, 10 years). Among the Italians the average age at first drink was about 8 years, 24% of the boys having tasted some form of alcohol by age 5 (34, *p. 64*).

Table wine was the first alcoholic beverage of 44% of the French respondents; of the rest 14% first tasted champagne, 11% cider, 9% an aperitif, 9% distilled spirits, and 7% beer. Wine was the first beverage primarily of children raised in the Southwest and Southeast, while those who lived in the Northwest more commonly tasted cider first, and those who lived in the Northeast were more likely

TABLE 29.—*Age at First Consumption of Alcohol and at First Intoxication, in Per Cent*

Age (years)	First Consumption			First Intoxication		
	Men	Women	Total	Men	Women	Total
1–3	6	5	6	0	0	0
4–6	20	18	19	2	1	1
7–9	18	14	16	3	3	3
10-12	20	21	20	11	7	9
13–15	11	11	11	16	8	12
16–18	6	7	7	25	12	19
19–21	2	3	2	20	8	14
More than 21	0	2	1	4	10	7
Never	0	0	0	8	32	20
No answer	18	19	18	11	19	15

to receive beer. Aperitifs were tasted first by many children in Paris and in the Southeast, and distilled spirits especially by those in the Northwest and Northeast.

The use of champagne in many of the first drinking experiences strongly suggested that they occurred during festive occasions. Further analysis revealed that they actually took place at a special ceremony—a wedding, an engagement party, a christening, a communion, or an anniversary—in 36% of the cases, at a local or national festival or during an unusual trip or vacation in 10%, as a childish prank in 7%, and during an ordinary family meal in 13%.

Childhood Drinking

Approximately half of the respondents occasionally drank wine mixed with water during childhood, especially between the ages of 8 and 12. Cider was the beverage most frequently used by 16% and beer by 10%. Water was nevertheless not unknown at French meals, since it was the beverage most frequently used during childhood by 24% of the respondents.

Only 5% of the boys and 3% of the girls drank undiluted wine regularly with meals, 14% of the boys and 10% of the girls occasionally drank an aperitif, and 11% of the boys and 5% of the girls distilled spirits.

Drinking in childhood was markedly influenced by the attitudes of the parents, and especially of the mothers. Unlike the Italian parents, who usually regarded the moderate use of wine by children as normal and unimportant (34), most French parents, as reported by the respondents, exhibited firm and often quite rigorous attitudes. Two-thirds of the parents were opposed—16% of them very strongly—to their children drinking alcohol in any form. At the other extreme, 6% were strongly in favor of such use and actually urged their children to drink wine, distilled spirits or other alcoholic beverages. Only about 11% of the parents seemed to have accepted early exposure to alcohol as a natural phase of child development.

Among the Italians, the fathers and mothers were characteristically agreed that moderate amounts of wine, usually diluted with water, were not dangerous for children. This attitude has apparently survived transplantation and the passing of generations and was obvious among third-generation Americans of Italian origin (34, *pp. 81-82*). Among French parents, however, agreement was less evident, the father sometimes strongly favoring early childhood drinking and the mother strongly opposing it.

The strictest control over childhood drinking in France, particularly by the mother, was reported by respondents in the Northeast and Northwest, those living in middle-sized or large communities, and those who now have high occupational status. In contrast, supervision was relatively lax during the childhood of those who grew up in rural areas, and those who are now manual laborers, farm owners or workers.

Interestingly, tight parental control during their childhood was more frequently reported by the relatively younger French subjects, especially those now below the age of 50, thus suggesting the growth of this tendency in more recent years.

First Excess in Drinking

Many of the respondents reported having been intoxicated or "drunk too much" on at least one occasion during childhood. The definition of intoxication, however, is difficult to establish. The term here is nontechnical and does not imply very high blood alcohol levels, though this undoubtedly occurred in some cases. Intoxication here means only sufficient drinking to cause a notable change in feeling, thinking or acting—a change which, if it had no or only slight consequences, was nevertheless not forgotten. Most of those who had "drunk too much" at least once in their early years reported it as a memorable event of their adolescence. In some, however, it had occurred relatively early in childhood.

As Table 29 shows, about one-fifth of the men and half of the women either had never been intoxicated or were unable to recall any details. Approximately 4% of the respondents reported first excessive drinking before age 10, while 40% (52% of the men and 27% of the women) had this experience between the ages of 10 and 18. It was recalled as happening at a family meal or celebration by 24%, during a meeting with friends by 11%, celebrating a twenty-first birthday or similar "emancipation" by 11%, as a childish exploit by 8%, during a local or national festival by 7%, "accidentally" by 6%, and during military service by 3%. In about half the cases the beverage involved was wine (table wine, 39%, and champagne, 13%), in 12% distilled spirits or liqueurs, in 10% aperitifs, and in 3% beer and in 3% cider.

Parental responses to this first intoxication were usually marked by amusement or indulgence, or by an indication that it was an uncomfortable but natural occurrence. Rarely did the parents make harsh judgments or ridicule the victim.

Among Italians an episode of excessive drinking during childhood occurred somewhat more frequently than among the French, being recalled as happening before the age of 10 by approximately 7%. These early experiences were generally associated with a party, festivity or religious holiday, when the child—without parental approval—drank wine beyond his capacity. In the overwhelming majority of such cases the event was not followed by parental censure or ridicule but was accepted as a painful educational experience for the child (34, *pp. 83, 85, 89*).

Adolescent Drinking

The interviews revealed that as they entered adolescence, French youth met a more tolerant attitude toward drinking alcoholic beverages. They could go out with friends unsupervised and, especially at the start of military service by the men, occasions to drink appeared more frequently, and the use of all alcoholic beverages increased markedly. The use of diluted wine at meals decreased or disappeared entirely, being replaced by other beverages. Between the ages of 14 and 18, straight wine was taken often by 27% of the men and 9% of the women, occasionally by 32% of the men and 25% of the women, and rarely by 23% of the men and 29% of the women.

Among Italians of comparable age the regular use of wine with meals was more commonly accepted, more than half of the boys and one-third of the girls having begun this practice before age 15 (34, *p. 130*).

Cider was used often by 22% of the French boys and 18% of the girls, occasionally by 12% of the boys and 13% of the girls, and rarely by 16% of both sexes. Beer was used often by 18% of the boys and 13% of the girls, occasionally by 20 and 14% respectively, and rarely by 20 or 21% of both sexes.

Between meals, usually at family gatherings, aperitifs were taken often by 9% of the boys and 3% of the girls, and occasionally by 35 and 23%, respectively. Similarly, distilled spirits—brandy and liqueurs —were used often by 8% of the boys and 2% of the girls, and occasionally by 28 and 14% respectively.

As shown in Table 30, these adolescent drinking habits marked a substantial change from those of childhood, with a steady increase in alcohol consumption. But where there had been only a slight difference in the behavior of boys and girls during childhood, the difference became marked after the age of 14.

As those of childhood, adolescent drinking habits were related to social environment and region. Again, "local" beverages—cider in the Northwest, and beer in the Northeast—were the most frequently used. Professionals, executives and white-collar workers reported a more restricted alcohol consumption during adolescence than farmers and manual laborers.

Regular as distinguished from occasional use of alcohol during adolescence was reported more frequently by the younger respondents—especially women—contrary to other indications of less drinking in recent years.

TABLE 30.—*Childhood and Adolescent Use of Alcoholic Beverages, by Beverage and Frequency, in Per Cent*

	MEN		WOMEN	
	Child-hood	Adoles-cence	Child-hood	Adoles-cence
Used Regularly with Meals				
Wine	5	27	3	9
Cider	18	22	14	18
Beer	12	18	9	13
Used Regularly between Meals				
Aperitif	14	9	10	3
Distilled spirits	11	8	5	2

During this period, new attitudes and preferences for specific beverages appeared, partly as the result of family environment and partly from the influence of other adolescents. As shown in Table 31, wine was surpassed by beer as the most popular beverage among adolescent boys while girls expressed particular preferences for sodas and coffee.

Sodas and coffee were most popular among adolescents in the larger cities, beer in the middle-sized and large cities, and wine and cider in small communities.

Related to the uses and choices of beverages were the leisure-time activities of these young people in sports, walks, dancing, movies, meetings with friends, and visits to cafés. Only 10% of these respondents (19% of the men, 2% of the women) reported very frequent visits to cafés during this period of their lives. As will be noted later (Chapter 5), frequency of this activity was reported by about half of a group of respondents who later became alcohol addicts.

Participation in athletics by boys was most common in the larger communities, probably because of greater availability of facilities. The preferred beverages of young men who engaged in sports were given as beer by 40%, sodas or fruit juice by 36%, wine by 18%, aperitifs by 12%, cider and distilled spirits each by 6%.

The preferred beverages of young men who participated mainly in walks, going to the movies, dancing, or meeting with friends, were reported as beer by 34%, wine by 31%, sodas or fruit juice by 24%, coffee by 21%, aperitifs by 13%, distilled spirits by 11%, and cider by 8%.

TABLE 31.—*Frequency of Drinking in Adolescence, by Preferred Beverage, in Per Cent*

Preferred Beverage	MEN			WOMEN		
	Often	Occasion-ally	Rarely	Often	Occasion-ally	Rarely
Beer	40	33	26	13	24	28
Wine	37	31	26	13	24	28
Sodas	27	23	26	58	37	16
Coffee	23	32	28	55	40	18
Aperitifs	12	33	37	3	19	30
Cider	12	12	27	10	14	21
Distilled spirits	11	32	33	2	16	28
Champagne	0	9	20	2	14	30

The preferred beverages of the adolescent boys whose main leisure activity was centered in cafés were reported as wine by 60%, beer by 35%, aperitifs by 29%, distilled spirits by 28%, coffee by 18%, cider by 9%, and sodas or fruit juices by 6%.

Among all groups of adolescent girls, nonalcoholic beverages—coffee, sodas and fruit juices—were always preferred. Among those young women who frequently went to a café, however, the customary use of alcoholic beverages was appreciable; aperitifs were listed as the preferred beverage by 19%, table wine by 14%, cider by 14%, beer by 10%, and distilled spirits and champagne each by 5%.

There appears to be a suggestion, in these data, of a relationship between adolescent drinking away from family groups—especially drinking in cafés—and the development of heavier drinking patterns.

Drinking in Military Service

At about age 20, many of the young men began a period of temporary military service. This event clearly constituted a transition from adolescence to adulthood, and for many of the respondents it marked an abrupt end of all family restrictions. This new freedom, together with opportunity to buy beverages at lower prices and the drinking traditions of military service—at the reception of recruits, promotions, various celebrations, and the return to civilian life—apparently led to an increased consumption of alcohol. Of the 87% of the men who had undergone military service, 45% reported they then drank more than before, usually wine, 30% the same amounts, and 10% less.

Increased drinking was reported particularly by those from the Northeast, those from communities with populations between 20,000 and 100,000, and those who later became white-collar workers and manual laborers. Only those who became executives and professionals indicated that they did not drink much more during military service but rather about the same amounts as before. The same respondents had also shown relatively more sober habits during childhood and adolescence than did the rest of the population.

Excessive Drinking in Adolescence

Three-fourths of the respondents reported no episodes of intoxication or only one such occurrence during adolescence. The remaining 25% (42% of the men and 7% of the women) reported excessive drinking to have occurred "several times." Table 32 shows that these excesses occurred most often during the adolescence of men who are now between the ages of 50 and 64, and among those who became manual workers, farm owners and farm hands.

In recalling and relating the circumstances of excessive drinking during childhood or adolescence, the respondents displayed neither embarrassment nor reticence, as these memories apparently involved obviously exceptional events.

Compared with childhood, in which drinking was in most cases strictly supervised, adolescence seemed to be a period of "new experiences" free from the taboos of the family, and an opportunity to experience full exposure to alcoholic beverages. In spite of this relative freedom, only a minority of the adolescents drank wine every day with meals, or frequently used aperitifs and brandy at celebrations, or visited cafés as the preferred type of entertainment. That the members of this minority might become excessive drinkers in adulthood if a psychological imbalance or environmental factors should intervene seems at least possible.

TABLE 32.—*Frequency of Excessive Drinking during Adolescence, by Present Age and Occupation, in Per Cent*

	Several Times	Once	Never
Age (Men)			
21–34	39	17	44
35–49	42	15	43
50–64	49	15	36
65+	37	16	47
Total	42	16	42
Age (Women)			
21–34	7	16	77
35–49	7	13	80
50–64	8	6	86
65+	4	3	93
Total	7	10	83
Occupation			
Farmer	34	13	53
Businessman	26	11	63
Professional, Executive	24	17	59
White collar	19	14	67
Manual	37	15	48

3. ADULT PATTERNS

The present section will describe the adult drinking practices of the respondents whose childhood and adolescent patterns have been detailed in the preceding section.

Beverage Preferences

As shown in Table 33, approximately half of the men and four-fifths of the women expressed a strong liking for coffee, tea and other hot drinks, and about one-fourth of the men and half of the women expressed a similar preference for sodas, fruit juices, mineral water and other cold nonalcoholic beverages.

Coffee and tea were preferred particularly by older respondents, while a taste for fruit juices and sodas—whose growing availability throughout France is a recent phenomenon—was characteristic of young men and even more so of young women. Hot beverages were about equally acceptable in all vocational groups and localities, while sodas and fruit juices were particularly popular in the larger cities and among the upper vocational groups.

Wine maintained its traditional place as the most widely preferred alcoholic drink, notably among farmers and manual laborers, followed by beer. As in other studies, men demonstrated a greater liking than women for nearly all forms of alcohol. Women expressed a particular approval of champagne and a particular dislike of distilled spirits.

The reasons for the lack of approval of distilled spirits among Frenchwomen—an attitude believed to be shared by women in other

TABLE 33.—*Adult Preferences for Alcoholic and Nonalcoholic Beverages, by Beverage, in Per Cent*

Beverage	Beverage Preferred		Beverage Accepted		Beverage Rejected	
	Men	Women	Men	Women	Men	Women
Coffee, tea	46	80	41	15	11	3
Sodas, juices, mineral water	26	57	35	31	35	9
Wine	70	33	24	48	5	16
Beer	50	24	37	36	11	35
Cider	24	20	33	33	36	37
Aperitif	35	21	47	44	15	31
Distilled spirits	26	10	39	32	33	54
Champagne	36	44	33	30	23	18

countries—are not completely clear. They may include a feminine dislike based on taste, the high cost of these beverages as a threat to the family budget, or the fear that these stronger alcoholic beverages may be dangerous as more intoxicating, or as a causative factor in excessive drinking or alcoholism.

Attitudes varied considerably with age. Wine and cider were preferred by men aged over 65, distilled spirits by those in the middle years, and beer and aperitifs by younger men. Among women, preferences for all forms of alcohol—even champagne—decreased steadily with age.

Drinking With and Between Meals

The significance of combining alcoholic beverages with food has been emphasized previously on physiological and psychological grounds (Chapters 1 and 2). In addition, French investigators have noted an apparent relationship between the rate of alcoholism in a specific area and the custom of drinking between meals. Thus in Marseille, where the rate of alcoholism is relatively low, drinking between meals is practiced habitually by only 2% of the men, whereas in St. Etienne, where the rate is relatively high, 55% drink between meals (6). Similarly among the Italians the use of alcohol is marked by a tradition of drinking with meals (34) and a low rate of alcoholism (19).

With Meals. Most of the respondents ate three or four times a day, generally breakfast, lunch and dinner plus a snack in the morning or afternoon. Most of them—about four-fifths—drank no alcoholic beverage of any kind with breakfast, while wine was the customary drink with lunch and dinner as well as during the extra snack. Mealtime consumption of alcoholic beverages other than wine was limited to certain occupational and regional groups, such as cider for farm owners and workers, or beer in the Northeast and cider in the Northwest.

Between Meals. In addition to the drinking with meals, 23% of the men and 6% of the women reported daily use of alcohol between meals and another 15 and 5%, respectively, reported frequent use. These respondents indicated a need or obligation to have a drink, at other than mealtimes, either alone or in the company of others, and at least 22% of these men and 36% of the women drank alone between meals. In contrast, only 2% of Italian men and 1% of Italian women preferentially used alcohol between meals (34, *p.* 72).

Of the French men who drank between meals, wine was taken by 45%, beer by 35%, cider by 12%, an aperitif by 9%, and distilled spirits by 2%. Of the women, most drank beer or wine, and a few cider or an aperitif.

These patterns were markedly affected by occupation. Between-meals drinking was most common among farm owners, farm hands and manual workers, and least among the retired. The beverages commonly used between meals by members of the different occupational groups are shown in Table 34. Farmers and heavy laborers attributed this use of alcohol primarily to "a need to drink," while businessmen and professionals generally explained it on the basis of "an occasion to drink."

Nonalcoholic beverages were drunk between meals mostly by women and by men in the upper occupational categories.

Drinking at Cafés

Much of the between-meal use of alcohol took place at cafés or bars, especially in Paris and other large cities. One out of 8 men (12%), but only 1 in 50 women, were accustomed to visiting a café every day; an additional 19 and 3%, respectively, several times a week; 19 and 9% several times a month; 34 and 33% rarely; and 16 and 53% never. It must be emphasized here again that a French café is not to be confused with an American cafe but is more comparable to an American bar or saloon, or a British pub. Food may or may not be available, but the major item for sale is always alcohol in one form or another. Drinking on an empty stomach is thus a major characteristic of café drinking. To a considerable extent, the French café is likewise the accepted meeting place for members of

TABLE 34.—*Adult Consumption of Alcohol Between Meals, by Occupation, in Per Cent*

Occupation	Wine	Beer	Cider	Aperitif	Distilled Spirits	Champagne
Farmers	43	13	29	2	2	
Businessmen	33	35	7	17	1	1
Professional, Executive	17	46	3	22	6	8
White collar	15	37	1	11	1	
Manual	45	37	4	9	2	
Retired	34	21	5	5	3	
Housewives	11	16	7	3		

the lower economic groups. In nearly every community, most workers have no other place in which to spend their leisure time (41, *p. 141*). For those in the lower economic groups as well as those with higher standards of living, drinking in a café may thus be considered the French equivalent of the American cocktail hour. In both instances alcohol is consumed without the protection of solid food, usually late in the day when fatigue and low blood sugar prevail, in the absence of the close-knit family group, and when the drinking seems to be primarily for psychological effect (28).

French authorities have long been aware of some of the hazards entailed in the large number of cafés and other outlets for alcoholic beverages (25, *pp. 69-78*). Efforts to reduce the number, however, have not met with wide popular support.

Visiting a café was primarily a habit of men, and especially of middle-aged men. It was a daily custom of about 12% of men aged between 21 and 49, 16% of those between 50 and 64, and 6% of those over 65; and of 3% of women aged between 21 and 34, 1% of those between 35 and 64, and none of those over 65. By marital status, daily visits to a café were made by 19% of the divorced, 9% of the single, 6% of the married, and 5% of the widowed. By occupations, shopkeepers and manual workers went to cafés most often, followed in frequency by white-collar workers, professionals and executives. Farmers were among the least frequent visitors, usually preferring to drink at home or at work.

Although it is possible to obtain nonalcoholic beverages at a café, these were rarely ordered by men. Of those who frequently patronized these establishments, wine was named as a preferred drink by 57%, beer by 34%, aperitifs by 24%, coffee or tea by 13%, and sodas or fruit juices by 9%. Of the relatively few women who visited cafés frequently, 46% expressed a preference for coffee, 31% for sodas or fruit juices, 31% for aperitifs, 23% for wine and 23% for beer.[1]

The foregoing data confirm some of the findings obtained in the study on consumption of alcoholic beverages (Chapter 1), particularly the relatively modest use of alcohol by women, the larger consumption of wine by farmers and heavy laborers, the preference of more expensive beverages such as aperitifs by the well-to-do, and the common use of wine at home and of aperitifs in a café.

---

[1] Multiple choices yield percentage totals above 100.

Excessive Drinking in Adult Life

Although the respondents evinced no particular reticence in describing instances of excessive use of alcohol during their childhood or adolescence, this was not true regarding such episodes in their adult life. Questions probing this area often drew evasive answers and the data obtained are at best approximate. It seems likely that some respondents underestimated the frequency of their excessive drinking bouts. Women seemed more evasive than men.

In the entire sample, 12% (21% of the men, 3% of the women) stated they had drunk too much "fairly often," and 55% (66% of the men, 43% of the women) only "rarely" or "exceptionally," while 30% (12% of the men, 50% of the women) reported they had never been intoxicated.

Table 35 shows that the largest proportions of those who drank too much "fairly often" were men in the age class 50–64, the divorced, manual workers or farmers, and inhabitants of the vicinity of Paris. Since the rate of heavy drinking is reportedly highest in the Northwest (25, *p. 143*), it is possible that the inhabitants of that region consistently underestimated the frequency of their drinking bouts in the present survey, perhaps by reference to a stricter criterion of excessive drinking.

When asked to estimate the number of times they had been intoxicated, almost one-fifth of the respondents were unable or unwilling to answer. The replies furnished by the others are shown in Table 36. The experience of five or more episodes of intoxication was reported by 20% of the entire sample. In 40% of the men and 11% of the women the last occasion of excessive drinking had taken place within the past year, and in 6% of the men and 1% of the women within the past week.

The occasions for excessive drinking cited most often were ceremonies or holiday meals with the family—already mentioned in connection with initial drinking and the first excessive use of alcohol —or outings and social gatherings with friends. Of those who provided information, 32% reported family celebrations as the commonest occasion for becoming intoxicated, 26% meetings with friends, 12% local or national festivals such as village fêtes, Bastille Day, or the Liberation Day of World War II. In 8% intoxication occurred mostly during army service, and in 4% at work, while 4% claimed that it happened without any particular occasion ("I was bored," "I was

TABLE 35.—*Frequency of Excessive Drinking in Adult Life, by Age, Marital Status, Occupation and Region, in Per Cent*

Age	Fairly Often	Rarely	Exception- ally	Never
Men				
21–34	16	31	36	15
35–49	22	35	30	12
50–64	30	30	31	8
65+	15	32	39	12
Total	*21*	*32*	*34*	*12*
Women				
21–34	2	10	38	47
35–49	2	10	36	47
50–64	2	11	30	51
65+	3	4	28	60
Total	*3*	*9*	*34*	*50*
Marital Status				
Single	13	18	32	34
Married, no children	15	20	35	27
Married, children	12	22	35	29
Widowed	9	15	27	44
Divorced	21	23	37	19
Occupation				
Farmer	17	23	28	29
Businessman	13	24	30	30
Professional, Executive	12	21	41	24
White collar	7	21	41	28
Manual	23	27	29	19
Retired	7	18	39	33
Housewife	1	11	36	49
Region				
Paris	19	23	30	27
Northwest	10	22	33	31
Northeast	10	19	40	27
Southwest	12	21	35	29
Southeast	11	19	29	39
Total	*12*	*21*	*34*	*30*

feeling blue," "It happens on Sundays"), and 6% that it happened accidentally.

Respondents (7% of the men and 1% of the women) who reported drinking to excess at work were mainly farm owners and farm hands. These were also the ones most likely to drink to excess for "no particular reason."

TABLE 36.—*Estimated Number of Excessive Drinking Episodes,
by Age, in Per Cent*

Age	None	1–2	3–4	5–14	15+
Men					
21–34	15	14	22	18	9
35–49	12	12	14	22	14
50–64	8	11	9	24	12
65+	12	18	15	17	9
Women					
21–34	47	25	13	7	2
35–49	47	20	15	6	1
50–64	51	17	12	9	1
65+	60	18	9	3	0
Total	*30*	*17*	*14*	*14*	*6*

The beverages involved in these episodes are shown in Table 37. Table wine was the beverage most often used, but it is noteworthy that aperitifs, distilled spirits and champagne, which constitute relatively small parts in the normal drinking of the French population, occupied relatively prominent roles in the excessive drinking of both men and women. That beverages other than wine figured relatively prominently in these periods of excessive drinking is presumably no coincidence. Although table wine offers alcohol in an appealingly inexpensive form, it is one which produces high blood-alcohol concentrations relatively slowly and thus fails to give the immediate psychological effects which may be desired. In addition, excessive drinking usually occurs not with meals but between meals, when little or no solid food is present in the stomach; under this condition the drinking of even moderate quantities of wine may cause local gastric irritation of such severity as to discourage further use—except, of course, in the case of addictive drinkers to whom the price has become of paramount importance.

TABLE 37.—*Beverages Used in Excessive Drinking Episodes, in Per Cent**

Beverage	Men	Women	Total
Wine	81	64	72
Beer	12	4	8
Cider	4	4	4
Aperitif	44	47	46
Distilled spirits	36	28	32
Champagne	22	53	38

* Totals more than 100% because of multiple answers.

Thus, excessive drinking in France was more widespread among men, took place mostly during home or local festivities or at social gatherings with friends, and involved not only table wine but relatively large amounts of aperitifs, distilled spirits and champagne.

Included in this cross-section of the population was a minority of respondents—a little less than 10%—whose excessive drinking took on a habitual aspect. This minority drank excessively without particular occasion, either at work or alone; it probably included real alcoholics.

A comparison of these patterns with those reported by Italians and Italian Americans (34, pp. 83-84) is especially interesting. Only 47% of the French respondents had experienced not more than two episodes of excessive drinking, compared to 68% of second- and third-generation Italian Americans and 83% of Italians in Italy. And five or more such episodes were reported by 20% of the French, 19% of the Italian Americans, and 10% of the Italians. It seems noteworthy in this connection that 19% of the French were unable or unwilling to offer any information on this subject, compared to less than 1% of the Italians or the Italian Americans. The beverages involved in these episodes of intoxication were exclusively wine for the Italians, mostly wine but also aperitifs, distilled spirits and champagne for the French, and mostly distilled spirits but also wine and beer for the Italian Americans.

4. THE ORIGIN OF DRINKING PATTERNS

The data recorded in the preceding sections on the childhood, adolescent and adult drinking habits of the French allow some consideration of the origin of these patterns. Some of these respondents appear to have shown tendencies in childhood and adolescence which foreshadowed their adult tastes and drinking customs. In others, however, there are no evident predictors.

In addition, by comparing the backgrounds of those who became moderate drinkers in adult life and those who became heavy drinkers, it may be possible to discover some of the personal factors involved in the development of excessive drinking.

Origin of Beverage Preferences

Adult tastes for beverages, either alcoholic or nonalcoholic, were seemingly determined mainly by social environment and region. In well-to-do circles, expensive beverages such as aperitifs or distilled spirits, or nonalcoholic drinks such as sodas and fruit juices (which are far from inexpensive in cafés), were generally preferred. In modest circles and in the rural areas, wine was the preferred beverage of adults, especially by manual workers and farmers, together with locally produced cider.

Adult tastes likewise seemed to differ with age. In contrast to respondents in their fifties, for example, young men and young women tended to prefer sodas, fruit juices and mineral water. But the preference for fruit juices and sodas may be an effect of increased availability, linked more to a general change in France than to a difference of taste based on age.

In addition to the influence exerted by geographical region and standard of living, the influence of the family was often equally important. As shown in Table 38, family influence manifested during childhood or adolescence tended to persist. For example, 52% of the adults preferred wine. In their childhood, their parents had always used wine with meals, and in their own adult life they also drank wine with meals. On the other hand, the 28% of the adults who preferred aperitifs and the 18% who favored distilled spirits were those who recalled the frequent use of these beverages at home during their adolescence or when they went out with friends. The childhood of these subjects was obviously spent in a family atmosphere in which the consumption of pure wine, aperitifs or distilled spirits by children was freely allowed.

Origin of Drinking with Meals

Adult habits of drinking with or between meals likewise seem to mirror customs established in childhood or adolescence. For example, of the 70% of the adults who customarily drank wine with

TABLE 38.—*Adult Preferences for Selected Beverages, by Adolescent Drinking Habits, in Per Cent*

	ADULT PREFERRED BEVERAGE[*]		
Adolescent Drinking	*Wine*	*Aperitif*	*Spirits*
Wine with meals with parental approval	15	17	18
Occasional aperitif with parental approval	16	23	23
Occasional distilled spirits with parental approval	12	15	22
Often aperitif during family gathering	9	14	16
Often distilled spirits during family gathering	8	10	22
Aperitif with friends	10	18	16
Distilled spirits with friends	8	10	19

[*] Wine preferred by 52% of all adults, aperitifs by 28%, and distilled spirits by 18%.

their noon meal, nearly all had been permitted to drink wine-with-water at meals during childhood and a few had been allowed to drink pure wine. In contrast, of the 11% of the adults who took little or no alcohol with lunch, two-thirds had drunk only water as children, a few had been permitted to drink wine-with-water, and none had used pure wine.

The adult use of alcoholic beverages at breakfast (by 11% of the sample) appears likewise to be related to drinking habits formed early. Of those who drank only water during childhood only 11% now drink an alcoholic beverage at breakfast, in contrast to 62% of those who were allowed wine-with-water in childhood, and 25 or 26% of those who had been allowed pure wine, aperitifs or distilled spirits.

Finally, drinking between meals—usually at a café or bar—is also related to childhood and adolescent customs. Table 39 shows a comparison of the childhood and adolescent drinking practices of two groups of respondents—those who practically never go to a café (34% of the sample) and those who go to them frequently to drink (13% of the sample). It is evident that substantially greater proportions of those who most frequently drink between meals in a café are those who were allowed or encouraged early to drink. The responses also showed that early preferences for beverages are

TABLE 39.—*Adult Café Drinking Habits, by Childhood and Adolescent Drinking, in Per Cent*

	Café Never*	Café Often†
Childhood Drinking		
Only water with meal	30	14
Wine-with-water with meal	39	52
Little pure wine with meal	6	24
Occasional aperitif	6	24
Occasional distilled spirits	4	21
Adolescent Drinking		
Often drank with meals	8	47
Among friends, often soda or fruit juice	52	17
Among friends, often coffee	51	15
Among friends, often wine	7	51
Among friends, often aperitif	2	23
Among friends, often distilled spirits	0	16
Often to café for distraction	2	35
Rarely to café for distraction	13	16

* 34% of all adults.   † 13% of all adults.

reflected in this style of adult drinking. Thus, those who frequently used wine during adolescence are more likely to drink wine in a café, while those who exhibited an early preference for nonalcoholic beverages tend as adults to avoid cafés.

Origin of Excessive Drinking

To gain some insight into factors which may be significantly involved in the development of dangerous drinking habits, two groups of respondents have been selected for particular examination: those who stated that they "drank too much" only occasionally or exceptionally—34% of the sample—here designated the "moderate drinkers"; and those who stated that they "drank too much" frequently—12% of the sample—here designated "excessive drinkers." Those who had never drunk to excess—nearly all of them women—are omitted from the present analysis. The general characteristics of the two groups are presented in Table 40.

TABLE 40.—*Moderate and Excessive Drinkers, by Sex, Age, Occupation and Residence, in Per Cent*

	Moderate Drinkers	Excessive Drinkers
Sex		
Men	51	90
Women	49	10
Age		
21–34	35	23
35–49	24	27
50–64	25	38
65+	16	12
Occupation		
Farmer	15	26
Businessman	7	8
Professional, Executive	3	2
White collar	21	10
Manual	20	45
Retired	14	7
Housewife	20	2
Residence (population)		
Under 2,000	32	36
2,000–5,000	13	10
5,000–20,000	17	17
20,000–100,000	16	8
Over 100,000	22	29
Percentage of all adults	*34*	*12*

Moderate Drinkers. These respondents, who reported that they liked some alcoholic beverages and used them moderately, included about the same proportions of men and women, and relatively large proportions of the young (59% under 50), white-collar workers, manual workers and housewives, and inhabitants of middle-sized communities.

Excessive Drinkers. This group presumably includes those who are addicted to alcohol, but it cannot be assumed that all or even many of these respondents were alcoholics, or that the size of the group represents the proportion of alcohol addicts in France. Most (90%) of these excessive drinkers were men. They include relatively large proportions of the older people, of farmers and manual laborers, and of those who lived in both the smallest and especially the very largest communities.

These characteristics conform to observations by others that the highest death rates from alcoholism are found among men, and notably men between the ages of 50 and 70 (25, *p. 136*). Regional investigations such as the study in Marseille also demonstrated a close relationship between excessive drinking and low standards of living as measured by poor housing (6). The more crowded the housing the greater was the average per capita consumption of total alcohol and the higher the proportion of persons who drank between meals.

Beverage Preferences. The moderate and excessive drinkers differed not only in the amounts of alcohol they consumed but also in their preferences for various beverages.

As Table 41 shows, the preferences for beer and cider were essentially equal in both groups. The moderate drinkers, however,

TABLE 41.—*Preferred Beverages of Moderate and Excessive Drinkers, in Per Cent*

Beverage	Moderate Drinkers	Excessive Drinkers
Sodas, fruit juice, mineral water	46	12
Coffee, tea, other hot beverages	65	34
Wine	48	92
Beer	44	42
Cider	22	22
Aperitif	28	51
Distilled spirits	15	46
Champagne	47	34

reported decidedly greater preferences for nonalcoholic drinks of all kinds, and a somewhat greater preference for champagne, while the excessive drinkers reported about twice as frequent preferences for wine and aperitifs, and three times more frequent preference for distilled spirits.

Drinking With Meals. An analysis of alcohol consumption at different times of the day is presented in Table 42. The vast majority of both groups drank with both lunch and dinner, but drinking with breakfast was reported by only 8% of the moderate, compared to 35% of the excessive drinkers. Drinking between meals as a frequent or daily custom was reported by 19% of the moderate but 72% of the excessive drinkers. Similarly, drinking often or daily at cafés was reported by 12% of the moderate and 57% of the excessive drinkers. Farm owners and farm workers reported frequent or daily drinking between meals but usually on the farm at work, rarely in cafés or similar establishments.

It is interesting to note that, nevertheless, 65% of the excessive drinkers did not drink at breakfast, 11% had no recollection of drinking between meals, and 26% said that they rarely or never went to a café.

In general, it appears that the excessive drinkers did not drink

TABLE 42.—*Drinking of Moderate and Excessive Drinkers, by Meal and Place, in Per Cent*

	Moderate Drinkers	Excessive Drinkers
Drinking with Meals		
Breakfast	8	35
Lunch	88	96
Dinner	87	87
Drinking between Meals		
Daily	8	51
Often	11	21
Occasionally	22	17
Never	27	4
No answer	32	7
Drinking at Café		
Daily	4	27
Several times a week	8	30
Several times a month	16	17
Rarely	40	21
Never	32	5

much more frequently at lunch and dinner, but they drank much more often at breakfast and especially between meals.

Childhood and Adolescent Drinking. During childhood, when drinking was strongly influenced by family custom, essentially the same drinking habits existed in the two groups with respect to most beverages. As shown in Table 43, water alone was used during childhood by 19% of the moderate drinkers and 17% of the excessive drinkers, and wine with water by 49% of the moderate drinkers and 41% of the excessive drinkers. Beer and cider were drunk by nearly the same proportions in each group. An exception is the drinking of undiluted wine by 2% of the moderate and 17% of the excessive drinkers, although the quantities are reported to have been quite small.

TABLE 43.—*Childhood and Adolescent Drinking Patterns of Moderate and Excessive Drinkers, in Per Cent*

	Moderate Drinkers	Excessive Drinkers
Childhood Drinking		
Only water with meals	19	17
Wine-with-water with meals	49	41
Little pure wine with meals	2	17
Beer with meals	12	11
Cider with meals	15	19
Other beverages	5	4
Age of First Intoxication		
1–3	0	0
4–6	2	2
7–9	6	6
10–12	11	18
13–15	11	29
16–18	24	26
19–21	21	11
Over 21	13	2
Unascertained	12	7
Excessive Drinking in Adolescence		
Several times	16	77
Once	23	6
Never	61	17
Drinking in Military Service (Men)		
Drank more	48	48
Drank same	25	26
Drank less	11	10
No service or no answer	16	16

By the end of childhood or the beginning of adolescence, however, definite differences are apparent. In many excessive drinkers, the first intoxication occurred at relatively earlier ages. By the age of 9, 8% of each group had been intoxicated. But between the ages of 10 and 15, 22% of the moderate and 47% of the excessive drinkers had experienced their first intoxication, and by the age of 18, 54% of the moderate and 81% of the excessive drinkers.

In the frequency of intoxication during adolescence, the patterns of the two groups show equally marked differences. During this period of life, when the subjects were more free to behave as they wanted, more than three-fourths of the excessive drinkers but only 16% of the moderate drinkers had been intoxicated, while 17% of the excessive and 61% of the moderate group reported no episodes of intoxication.

At the same time, in their adolescent leisure-time activities, those who were to become moderate drinkers were more inclined to participate in athletics or in dances, walks, going to the movies and similar social affairs, while those who later became excessive drinkers were already spending much of their time in cafés and other establishments where alcohol was readily available.

There is no indication to suggest that the moderate drinkers avoided cafés and bars during their adolescence because of financial or other economic reasons. Most of them came from families with relatively high standards of living, and were able to purchase expensive alcoholic beverages if they preferred them.

It is also obvious that, in their childhood and adolescence, the future moderate drinkers were not rigid abstainers. They drank non-alcoholic beverages, but they also drank alcoholic beverages, particularly wine and beer. When they used alcohol, they used it primarily in these relatively dilute forms and always in moderation. They drank almost entirely with meals, when potential hazards were moderated by the presence of food in the stomach. And, perhaps as the result of family influences early in childhood, they found no particular pleasure or elevated social status in drinking to excess.

It seems, therefore, that the behavior of respondents who became excessive drinkers as well as that of those who developed more moderate habits is foreshadowed by earlier drinking patterns. The adult patterns thus appear to reflect not so much the present availability, pricing or advertising of alcohol, as the influences of regional traditions, social factors and, particularly, family customs, all exerted very early in life. It is these latter influences which seem to play the most significant role in determining the drinking patterns of France.

5. SUMMARY

The drinking patterns of French adults (aged over 20) were studied in an interview survey of a stratified sample of the national population during July and August 1959.

1. The average age at first taste of alcohol in any form was 9.7 years. The commonest beverage at first drink was table wine (44%), and the commonest occasions were a special party, festival or other event, or a childish prank. In 13% it occurred as part of a normal family meal. Between age 8 and 12, about half of the sample occasionally drank wine mixed with water, 16% cider, and 10% beer; 4% received undiluted wine regularly with meals. About 4% had drunk to excess before age 10, and 40% had been intoxicated at least once between ages 10 and 18.

2. Two-thirds of the parents of the respondents were strongly opposed to any use of alcoholic beverage in childhood (mothers most frequently and strongly), while 6% were strongly in favor; about one-tenth of the parents were remembered as accepting childhood drinking as normal. The strictest parental control over childhood drinking was reported in the Northeast and Northwest; the strongest parental approval was reported in rural areas, and by manual laborers and farmers.

3. During adolescence, wine was used regularly by 27% of the men and 9% of the women as mealtime beverages, cider by 22 and 18%, and beer by 18 and 13%, while between meals, aperitifs were used regularly by 9% of the men and 3% of the women, and distilled spirits by 8 and 2%. Excessive drinking occurred during adolescence at least "several times" in 25% (men 42%, women 7%), especially among manual workers, farm owners and farm hands. Adolescent drinking away from family groups—especially drinking in cafés—was closely related to the development of heavier drinking patterns. In men, the period of military service was often marked by a substantial increase in alcohol consumption.

4. Among men, wine and cider were preferred particularly by those over age 65, distilled spirits by those in the middle years, and beer and aperitifs by the younger respondents. More than one-third of the men and one-tenth of the women drank frequently between meals, particularly farm owners, farm hands and manual laborers. Drinking at a café every day or several times a week was reported by nearly one-third of the men and one-twentieth of the women. Daily café visits were reported by 19% of the divorced, 9% of the single, 6% of the married, and 5% of the widowed.

5. About half of the sample reported not more than two episodes of intoxication during their lifetime, but five or more such episodes were

reported by 20%. Aperitifs, distilled spirits and champagne, which played a relatively minor part in the normal drinking of adults, occupied relatively prominent roles in the excessive drinking of both men and women, but table wine was the most often used beverage. Excessive drinking by adults appeared to be related to regional factors, socioeconomic factors, parental drinking habits and attitudes, drinking between meals beginning in childhood or adolescence, drinking outside the family circle during adolescence, and frequent excessive drinking during adolescence.

6. Two selected groups were compared: excessive drinkers, those who stated that they often drank too much (12% of the sample), and moderate drinkers, those who stated they rarely drank too much (34% of the sample). The moderate drinkers included equal proportions of men and women but more (59%) under age 50, white-collar workers, manual workers and residents of middle-sized communities, while the excessive drinkers were men (90%) and included more older people, farmers and manual workers, and residents of the smallest and largest communities. More excessive than moderate drinkers (35% and 8%) drank with breakfast, visited cafés daily or often (57% and 12%), were given undiluted wine in childhood (17% and 2%). By age 15, 30% of the moderate and 55% of the excessive drinkers had been intoxicated, and by age 18, 54 and 81%. During adolescence 61% of the moderate but only 17% of the excessive drinkers did not become intoxicated.

7. Comparison of the drinking patterns of the French, with a high reported rate of alcoholism, and that of Italians, with a low rate, shows the following: (a) Average age at first drink: French, 9.7 years, Italians, 8; (b) beverage at first drink: French, wine in less than half, Italians, wine in nearly all; (c) first childhood drink as part of normal family meal: French, 13%, Italians, 83%; (d) childhood drinking, even in extremely dilute form, unemotionally accepted by about 10% of French parents and nearly all Italians; (e) occurrence of excessive drinking before age 10: French, 4%, Italians, 7%; (f) regular use of alcohol between meals during adolescence: French, more than one-fourth, Italians, practically none; (g) in adult life, wine, beer, cider, aperitifs, distilled spirits and champagne all consumed in substantial amounts by the French, wine used almost exclusively by the Italians; (h) occurrence of not more than two episodes of intoxication reported by 47% of the French and 83% of the Italians, five or more such episodes by 20% of the French and 10% of the Italians.

Chapter 5

THE DRINKING PATTERNS OF ALCOHOLICS

1. INTRODUCTION

THE DIFFERENCES between moderate drinkers and alcoholics are, in France as in other countries, painfully apparent. In contrast to those who can drink safely and even beneficially, the alcoholics consume alcohol in excessive quantities, are frequently intoxicated, and create problems for their families and friends, the medical profession, the police, and even the government. These characteristics of alcoholics, however, may well be likened to the symptoms of a disease in an advanced stage. An examination of these symptoms casts little light on the factors which caused them. Similarly, study of the present condition of alcoholics offers little help in determining the factors which protect the great majority of drinkers from excesses. Instead, it appears more useful to examine the background of alcoholics, going back as far as possible into their childhood and adolescence, to study their drinking histories and the origin of their drinking patterns.

Such a survey was conducted as a part of the present study of the role of drinking in French culture.[1] Interviews were obtained from 120 alcoholics selected from four major sections (See Map 1): (a) the departments of Finistère and Côtes-du-Nord in Brittany; (b) the department of Orne in Normandy; (c) Paris; and (d) the departments of Gard and Hérault in Languedoc in the Midi.

While the use of many different alcoholic beverages is common in Paris, both Brittany and Normandy are noted for a high consumption of apple cider and apple brandy, and the Midi is characterized by a very high consumption of wine.

No subjects were drawn from the northeastern areas of France, where beer is a major beverage. Accordingly, these findings cannot be taken as a complete reflection of the drinking patterns of all French alcoholics. Furthermore, the size and nature of the sample make it obvious that the results do not necessarily indicate the drinking habits and attitudes of all alcoholics in France, or in the

---

[1] A preliminary and abbreviated report of the findings has been presented by Sadoun and Lolli (44).

106

specific areas considered here. Nevertheless the data are believed to illustrate adequately the striking differences between alcoholics and the normal or moderate users of alcohol in France.

All the subjects were unquestionably alcohol addicts as defined by contemporary workers in the field. They were selected for this study on the basis of criteria developed in cooperation with the Centre Psychiatrique de Ville-Evrard and the Centre Psychiatrique de Villejuif in Paris. They were contacted, diagnosed and interviewed in their customary environments—mostly bars, cafés and other public places licensed to sell alcoholic beverages. The interviews were conducted by trained personnel between September and December 1959.

Description of Sample

Sex. The group consisted of 115 men and 5 women. There is no indication that this ratio represents the sex distribution of alcoholics in France.

Age. The ages ranged from 16 to 75 years, distributed as follows: 16–19 years, 1%; 20–34, 19%; 35–49, 48%; 50–64, 24%; 65–75, 8%.

Region. By regions they were distributed as follows: Brittany, 17%; Normandy, 14%; Paris, 52%; the Midi, 17%. Most of the alcoholics lived in cities—including Nîmes, Alençon, Flers, Douarnenez and Paris—4% residing in communities with less than 2,000 population, 4% in those between 2,000 and 5,000, 21% in those between 5,000 and 20,000, 10% in those between 20,000 and 100,000, and 61% in those with more than 100,000.

Education. Educational status was distributed as follows: No formal education, 6%; completed primary school, 61%; upper primary school, 9%; secondary school, 14%; technical school, 2%; college or university, 6%; unascertained, 2%. The educational level was typical of the general population. It was noted that some of the subjects had wanted to continue their studies but had failed in examinations.

Occupation. There were few professionals or other high occupations but a fairly large number of manual laborers, vagrants and unemployed. The distribution of occupations was as follows: manual workers, including unskilled, farm workers and unemployed, 21%; skilled, 28%; white-collar, 27%; small tradesmen or shopkeepers, 18%; executives, professionals and business owners, 6%. Included in the last category were a business executive, an antiquarian, a pharmacist and an assistant bank director, evidence that in France as in other countries not all addicts are impoverished, jobless habitués of Skid Row.

Military Service. Approximately one-eighth of the group had been or were presently "with the army." Many of these indicated they had never made satisfactory adjustments to normal civilian life. Most of these men had belonged to such special units as the Foreign Legion, the colonial troops or the Africa Battalions.

Criminal Records. A large portion—17%—had been in what was described as "in contact with the police." The true percentage of delinquents was probably higher, but this subject was not systematically investigated by the interviewers and this type of information was not always volunteered. The incidents ranged in importance from a brief stay at the local police station to imprisonment for murder.

Marital Status. The abnormal marital status noted in other groups of alcoholics (9, 29, 40, 51) was observed also in this group of French subjects: 53% were married and living with their spouses, 19% divorced or separated, 6% widowed, and 22% single. This distribution is in striking contrast with that of the general French population (Chapter 1). Of those subjects who described themselves as married and living with their spouses, approximately three-quarters reported "unhappy marriages" and "regular scenes."

These findings—especially the very large percentage of adults who had never married, even though their excessive drinking may have been only a recent development—support the belief that not only does alcoholism lead to broken marriages, but that some alcoholics-to-be may possess personality traits which prevent marriage.

The number of children of the subjects was reported as follows: none, 21%; 1 or 2, 47%; 3 or 4, 14%; 5 or 6, 5%; 7, 1%; no information, 12%.

Drinking History of Parents. A remarkably high proportion of the parents of these subjects were described by them as alcoholics. About 73% reported that one or both of their parents were alcoholics, and an additional 8% were unable or unwilling to provide information on this point. Usually only the father was described as an excessive drinker, though in a few cases both parents were so termed. In every case in which the mother was depicted as an alcoholic, the father was described in the same way. It was not possible to determine whether or not some of the subjects were consciously or unconsciously protecting an idealized mother-image in avoiding a description of her as intemperate.

Judgments on the alcoholism of the father were relatively mild and commonly it was excused on grounds such as "hard work." Moreover, the alcoholic father was rarely described as brutal; although he might occasionally slap his wife or children, and was sometimes given to violence, he was pictured as mostly a good father and a good husband, who brought home his pay and tried to provide for his family.

The greater overindulgence in alcohol attributed by these alcoholics to their fathers may also be due in part to the relatively low economic level of most of the families. With a limited income, the alcoholic beverage was an expensive food reserved primarily for the father who would thus be the heaviest consumer.

By region, at least one alcoholic parent was reported by 92% of the subjects in Normandy, 75% of those in Brittany, 70% of those in the Midi, and 54% of those in Paris.

Treatment for Alcoholism. At the time of the study, none of the subjects was in a hospital or rehabilitation center. In the past, only 7 of the 120 had undergone any medical treatment for alcoholism. Of these latter, only 2 had voluntarily requested treatment; the others had either been sent to a psychiatric hospital after an episode of violence or of severe delirium tremens, or had sought treatment after an accidental injury or the threat of divorce, arrest or loss of a job.

Approximately three-fourths of the subjects claimed to be in good health, and most denied they were alcoholics. Without attempting to analyze the reasons for his current condition, the average subject usually took pains to explain that he was undoubtedly a heavy drinker who liked only healthy and natural alcoholic beverages, who handled them well and felt better when he drank than otherwise, but that he should not be confused with an alcoholic. But these men never specified clearly in which way they differed from true alcoholics, except for the notion that they possessed a superior tolerance.

2. USE OF ALCOHOL

Daily Consumption

As expected, the use of alcohol by the members of this group was excessive. Their average daily consumption, by self-report, was as follows: wine, 2,500 cc., beer, 41 cc.,[2] cider, 10 cc., wine-based aperitifs, 100 cc., nonwine-based aperitifs, 260 cc., and distilled spirits, 40 cc. This intake equals approximately 250 cc. of ethyl alcohol from wine, 1.6 cc. from beer, 0.4 cc. from cider, 17 cc. from wine-based aperitifs, 52 cc. from nonwine-based aperitifs, and 20 cc. from distilled spirits (usually grape or apple brandy), a total of 341 cc. of absolute alcohol. This is close to the alcohol content of an American "fifth" of 90-proof whisky.

The lowest daily consumption, reported by a Parisian alcoholic, was 1500 cc. of red wine with his meals, 1,000 cc. of beer, and 2 glasses of aperitif wine, giving a total of 210 cc. of alcohol. It is noteworthy that this amount of alcohol is less than the upper limits reported by 2% of all men in the general population, who consumed between 200 and 299 cc. of absolute alcohol during a 24-hour period, while 1% drank more than 300 cc. (Chapter 1).

The highest consumptions were reported by an alcoholic in Hérault who stated he drank 4 liters of wine and 20 anisette aperitifs daily, equivalent to 800 cc. of absolute alcohol; a Finistère alcoholic who drank 9 liters of wine daily, equivalent to 900 cc. of alcohol; and an Orne alcoholic, who declared he drank 6 liters of wine, 10 glasses of aperitifs, and about a liter of apple brandy daily, totaling nearly 1000 cc. of alcohol. The reliability of these claims is unknown.

Intoxication. The drinking of these alcoholics was steady and regular as well as excessive. Their consumption apparently knew no respite, and not one individual among them reported a cyclical or intermittent drinking pattern. Under these conditions, it is hardly surprising that 51% of the subjects stated that they were intoxicated fairly often, including 31% who reported being intoxicated every day and 8% about once a month. But 16% of the alcoholics claimed they were never intoxicated, and 27% described only rare or exceptional episodes.

[2] As noted in the preceding section, none of the subjects in this group was selected from the northeastern sections of France where the use of beer is most common.

The continued excessive drinking may be explained in large part by the almost omnipresent consumption of alcoholic beverages—particularly wine—at the table. Since consumption between meals was added to the drinking with meals, most of these subjects were in a permanent state of alcoholization.

The time of drinking, however, appeared to affect the selection of beverage. Thus, about 97% of the aperitifs, 73% of the distilled spirits, 56% of the wine and 6% of the cider were consumed between meals and probably on an empty stomach.

Beverages. Selection of beverages was decidedly influenced by region. In Brittany, for example, the alcoholics clearly preferred red wine, particularly the gros bleu of Algeria, introduced by the tuna fishermen of Mauritania and, since World War I, drunk almost exclusively along the coast of France. This is a heavy, almost purple wine, with an alcohol content of 12 to 13%. It has a very ordinary taste and, except in Brittany, is usually diluted with water.

In Normandy cider was preferred by the alcoholics, but it was beginning to be replaced by red wine in spite of the higher price of the latter as a source of alcohol. The most favored beverage of the region, however, was apple brandy (calvados).

In the south of France, the Midi alcoholics preferred rosé wine and anisette aperitifs. Red wine was used with meals, the other beverages frequently between meals.

In Paris the picture was more varied. Red wine was preferred, followed in order by white and rosé, wine-based aperitifs, and various forms of distilled spirits.

Whatever the region, the alcoholics rarely expressed an exclusive preference based solely on "taste." Their preferences were influenced by taste, alcohol content, price, custom, pleasant or unpleasant effects of the beverage, and its reputation as a "natural" or "manufactured" product. The commonest influence, however, was economic. The alcoholic who regularly drinks to excess must obviously watch his expenditures. But this does not always blunt his taste, nor his memory of better drinks. This largely explains why most of the alcoholics expressed preferences for many different beverages, but usually settled for red wine, which is always accessible at low cost by the liter or glass.

In addition, many alcoholics, forced for one reason or another to turn to unpalatable beverages, ultimately develop strong likings for these unfamiliar drinks. This was noted, for example, in subjects who had seen military service in Indochina or Africa and had become acquainted with such native beverages as rice alcohol, shoum, and fig alcohol, first with distaste but then with considerable relish.

Drinking Patterns

First Exposure. Nearly a third of the subjects were unable to recollect their first drink and stated they had "always" used alcohol or had been drinking for "a long time." The others gave their age at first drink as follows: 3–4 years, 10%; 5–10, 26%; 11–15, 26%; 16–20, 8%; and 21–25, 1%. Thus in about half of those able to recall their age at first drink, it was 10 years or less. The comparable proportion in the entire population of France is about the same (Chapter 4). In the Italian population, about 60% had been introduced to an alcoholic beverage by that age, and 20% had first tasted an alcoholic beverage by the age of 5 (*34, p. 64*).

The beverage in the first experience of the French alcoholics was wine for 48%, cider for 17%, an aperitif for 5%, distilled spirits for 4% and beer for 3%. The others were unable to recall.

During childhood, between ages 8 and 12, undiluted wine was commonly drunk with meals by 14% of these subjects, wine with water by 26%, cider by 21%, beer by 4%, distilled spirits by 2%, and water was used with meals by 26%. In Normandy, cider and apple brandy were the only alcoholic beverages used with meals by these subjects as children, while wine—either undiluted or mixed with water—was the only form of alcohol used in the Midi.

The drinking of beverages with a high alcohol content during childhood was particularly prevalent in Normandy. There, generally by age 3 or 4, the child stopped drinking milk and turned to low-alcohol cider, but soon thereafter was allowed a calvados or apple brandy once or twice a month.

Parental Attitudes. Parental attitudes towards early introduction to alcohol were notably rigid, with roughly two-thirds of the parents of these subjects approving and one-third disapproving. A dispassionate or unemotional acceptance of this experience as a normal event was essentially unknown. These rigid attitudes, with emphasis on the benefits or the hazards of alcohol, are in marked contrast to those of Italian parents, who accept childhood exposure to alcohol without particular feelings but as a normal experience in child development (34, *p. 81*).

One-third of the French alcoholics recalled that parental supervision of early drinking had been very strict. This control was especially evident in the Midi, where 50% of the parents reportedly supervised the drinking of their children, and least in Brittany and Normandy. In some homes the children were freely permitted or even encouraged to use alcoholic beverages.

The form of parental supervision was markedly affected by the parental drinking patterns. When one or both parents was an alcoholic—reported by three-fourths of the alcoholics—only 26% watched over the child's drinking; when neither parent was an excessive drinker, 80% did. But even among the alcoholic parents, one-third supervised the drinking habits of their children to some extent. This was true particularly in the case of nonalcoholic wives of alcoholic husbands. In such homes the supervision was often as strict as that of abstaining parents.

These variations in parental noninterference and strictness, which may be related to the alcoholism of the children, seemed to stem from different factors. Apart from the case in which the nonalcoholic wife sought to protect her children by strict supervision (to which the alcoholic father usually remained indifferent), a number of alcoholic fathers also took active responsibility. These fathers, generally from the lower middle or middle class, would behave circumspectly at the table, rigidly control their children's drinking, and try to keep up the appearances of sobriety.

First Intoxication. The age at first excessive alcohol consumption was reported by the alcoholics as follows: 4–6 years, 2%; 7–9, 2%; 10–12, 6%; 13–15, 26%; 16–18, 37%; 19–21, 15%; over 21, 12%. Comparison with the reports of the general population (Chapter 4) shows that those who became moderate drinkers tended to have this experience relatively earlier and, thereafter, were less inclined to repeat it.

The first episode of intoxication occurred during a family celebration in 17%, at a local celebration in 7%, an outing with friends in 17%, during military service in 19%, and at work in 15%. In the general population the first experience of overindulgence occurred most often during a family celebration.

The first occurrence of intoxication described by the alcoholics rarely had parental sanction or acceptance. It was sometimes the object of ridicule by the father, who claimed his son "couldn't hold his liquor."

The beverage involved in this first episode was wine in about half the cases and either distilled spirits or an aperitif in most of the others.

Adolescent Patterns. Parental control over drinking usually disappeared when the subject started to work. By age 14 or 15 many of the subjects had become apprentices, factory workers or laborers. Then, and particularly among such heavy laborers as farmers, construction workers and quarriers, daily consumption of alcohol increased markedly.

During adolescence, and especially between ages 14 and 18, wine was used commonly by 54%, aperitifs by 44%, beer by 25%, distilled spirits by 15%, and cider by 4%, while the common use of sodas or fruit juices was reported by only 23% and coffee by only 4%. In the national population, wine was used commonly by 16% of adolescents, aperitifs by 6%, beer by 19%, distilled spirits by 4%, cider by 8%, sodas or fruit juices by 27% and coffee by 25% (Chapter 4).

Approximately half of the alcoholics, in contrast to one-tenth of the general population, reported frequent visits to cafés and other establishments selling alcoholic beverages. Only 21% participated frequently in dances, 12% in sports, 6% in meetings with friends, 5% in walks, and 3% in attending theaters or movies.

The beginnings of heavy drinking seem evident during the adolescent period. Approximately two-thirds of the alcoholics—in contrast to one-fourth of the general population—reported that excessive drinking or intoxication had already occurred "several times."

Some of the alcoholics related their later excessive consumption to a steady increase of daily drinking beginning in childhood and continuing during adolescence. This was noted particularly among young farm workers from alcoholic families in Normandy. Others who had been rigidly supervised as children and had shown no particular liking for alcoholic beverages, said that their entry into vocational life was marked by an abruptly imposed form of excessive drinking. As apprentices or young workers they were literally forced to undergo an initiation ritual based on alcohol. Older workers openly led them to drinking, and even forced them to drink, to prove their membership in the group and to demonstrate their manhood. These drinking ceremonies were almost invariably climaxed by intoxication and thereafter the daily intake—actively directed by the older workers—steadily increased until the novices could demonstrate their virility and their right to acceptance.

Even some fathers of the subjects took part in this enforced drinking. For example, one subject stated: "I started at 14. I was not in Paris any more, but in the quarries. I cut stones with my father. At 14, I drank my liter of wine during work. So did my father. . . . Me, I had my half-liter mug at work. We had a liter for the two of us in the morning, and, in the afternoon, a liter during work. My father started me off like that. If I had not wanted to drink, he would have punched me in the face. So I drank, and I will drink until I die."

Occupationally Related Drinking. To such forms of initiation were added traditional contributions by some employers, many workers receiving a substantial amount of alcohol as part of their wages (41, *p. 184*). For example, in western France the delivery of vegetables to receiving stations entitled a worker to a certain number of liters of wine per loaded wagon. Workers in smelters and foundries received free issues of 3 to 5 liters of wine for 8 hours of work. Many building contractors customarily issued a 20-liter ration of wine to a working gang. On fishing boats, wine or rum was often provided as part of the work contract. In the fields, especially at harvest time, the landowner customarily provided alcoholic beverages to the workers.

Still another form of occupationally related excessive drinking was reported not only in adolescents but also among adults in such groups as truck drivers, cooks, hotel waiters and traveling salesmen. Thus, working at night and stopping regularly to make deliveries appeared to contribute to excessive drinking by truck drivers. The constant accessibility of alcoholic beverages in restaurants, cafés and bars was said to be a strong influence on waiters and barmen. Traveling salesmen emphasized the importance of ordering drinks at the right moment to get business. For owners of bars or restaurants who feel obligated to drink with customers, progressive alcoholization appears to be an occupational hazard.

Drinking in Military Service. Many subjects reported beginning their excessive drinking during their period of temporary military service at the end of adolescence, usually after the age of 20. Slightly more than 40% of the alcoholics reported that they drank more while in the service and only 1% drank less. The reasons for this excessive consumption were invariably given as idleness, boredom and, particularly, the lack of recreational distractions. Many of the recruits were stationed in remote provinces or small towns which offered no entertainment except an occasional movie and a Sunday dance, but were invariably well-supplied with cafés, bars and brothels. Whether the soldier drank in the cantine of his own barracks or in a café, alcohol seemed the only recourse in a situation of bewilderment and lack of recreation.

Somewhat related were the factors associated with the excessive drinking of professional soldiers, particularly of such special troops as the Foreign Legion, the Africa Battalions, the Marines and the colonial troops. Sixteen of the 120 alcoholics in this sample had served with such units. In these specialized corps, excessive drinking was apparently more pronounced than in the regular Army. This type of drinking was often attributed to climatic conditions—in the colonies, for instance. But it may be linked to the personal characteristics of men who join these special troops. Especially veterans of service in Asia and Africa during World War II or more recently, reported the ingestion of generous rations of rum, grape brandy, rice brandy or date brandy—as much as 750 cc. per day—and progressively increasing daily consumption of all alcoholic beverages.

Alcoholic Episodes. In their present drinking episodes, as shown in Table 44, most of the alcoholics used wine in all phases of the bout. In other cases, as the episode progressed, there was a marked decrease in the use of aperitifs and an increase in the consumption of beer and distilled spirits.

TABLE 44.—*Beverages Preferred and Used by Alcoholics, in Per Cent*

Beverage	Preferred*	Used During Intoxication		
		Onset	Peak	End
Wine	82	64	73	62
Beer	15	3	11	15
Cider	2	3	0	0
Aperitifs	31	21	5	5
Distilled spirits	24	9	11	18

* Total more than 100% because of multiple answers.

3. SUMMARY

1. Interviews were obtained with 120 alcohol addicts from four regions of France—Brittany, Normandy, Paris and the South. The subjects were contacted in their customary environment, mostly drinking places. Only 53% were married and living with spouse, 19% were divorced or separated, 6% were widowed and 22% were single. Nearly three-fourths had at least one parent who was an alcoholic.

2. About half of those who remembered had had their first drink before age 10—approximately the same proportion as in the general population. About one-third of the parents disapproved of this early initiation and two-thirds approved; few accepted it unemotionally. In the national population, about two-thirds of the parents disapproved of this early introduction, and one-tenth strongly approved.

3. The first intoxication occurred before age 13 in 10% of the alcoholics, and in 18% of the national population.

4. The adolescence of many future alcoholics was marked by frequenting of cafés, initiation "rituals" in which apprentices and young workers were forced to drink to intoxication to prove their virility, provision of alcoholic beverages by employers as partial wages, and increasing occurrence of drunken episodes. Others commenced excessive drinking during military service at the end of adolescence.

5. Both early drinking habits and present drinking preferences were substantially affected by regional characteristics, but wine was the most frequently used beverage of approximately half the alcoholics. Their daily mean average consumption of absolute alcohol was about 340 cc. The lowest daily consumption reported by any individual was equivalent to 210 cc. of alcohol, the highest, nearly 1,000 cc.

6. Excessive consumption was the common daily practice, including drinking at and between meals so that the subjects were under the influence of alcohol almost permanently. No subject reported an intermittent drinking pattern. Over 50% reported being intoxicated fairly often, 31% every day.

7. During drinking episodes wine, the cheapest form of alcohol available, was used by a majority of the subjects, but some shifted to greater use of beer and distilled spirits as the alcoholic episode progressed.

Chapter 6

THE PREVENTION OF ALCOHOLISM

THE RESULTS of the five related inquiries presented here—in particular, the data on actual consumption, public and medical attitudes, and the factors involved in the development of drinking patterns—provide some useful illumination on the role of alcohol in French culture, and offer some insight into the origins and the progression of excessive drinking in France. The findings, however, have implications which reach far beyond the interests of the French people. Their greatest significance lies in their applicability to the understanding of drinking problems in many countries.

Clearly, the knowledge of comparative drinking patterns has values which transcend national borders. This has been evident since the recognition that alcohol problems are rare in some cultures and frequent in others, but that their absence or prevalence is not related simply to the relative quantities of alcoholic beverages that the members of a culture drink.

The comparative drinking patterns of the Italians, the French and the Americans are notably revealing. The per capita alcohol consumption of the Italians is second only to that of the French, and much greater than that of the Americans (10, *Table 8*), and yet the rate of alcoholism in Italy is evidently far lower than in France or the United States (10; 19; 22, *Table 2*).

Since the relative immunity of the Italians to the hazards of alcoholism could not be attributed to abstinence, considerable effort has been devoted to a search for the features which may have enabled these people to use alcohol safely and even beneficially (32-35, 45, 57). From some of these investigations, a cluster of factors which seem to be associated with the reasonably safe drinking of most Italians has been identified (34). Among them, perhaps the most important is the traditional Italian custom of viewing alcohol in the form of wine as a food, and drinking wine exclusively or almost exclusively with meals. The small proportion of Italians who fall prey to alcoholism may or may not drink with their meals, but invariably they drink abundantly between meals (29). This finding in turn has stimulated research in the laboratory, aimed at

118

clarifying the physiological, psychological and social factors which may contribute to the safety inherent in the alimentary uses of wine. Thus it has been demonstrated by a battery of physiological and psychological measurements that, for instance, 10 oz. of wine taken with a meal by a 150-pound man will produce essentially the same blood-alcohol level as 5 oz. taken on an empty stomach, and that—even with identical blood-alcohol levels—the effects of wine on the central nervous system are more marked when taken on an empty stomach than when taken on a full stomach (13, 30, 35, 45).

The presence of food in the body, especially if it includes the slowly absorbable carbohydrates typical of the Italian diet, likewise helps to prevent low or fluctuating blood sugar levels and this may aid in protecting the central nervous system from some of the toxic effects of alcohol (12). But perhaps of equal importance is the circumstance that drinking with meals is usually an experience shared by the family, forming an intimate and mutually controlling group. On the other hand, the consumption of alcoholic beverages apart from food appears to be linked with a search for psychological rather than physiological effects of alcohol (34, *p.* 73).

The physiological protection provided by the dietary use of alcohol—as in the drinking of wine with meals—has evidently been known and understood intuitively in Italy for many centuries. It has been less appreciated in modern France, and this may be one factor largely responsible for the remarkable difference between the alcoholism rates of the two countries.

A comparison of the previously reported findings on the Italians and other groups with those presented here on the French reveals a number of important differences:

1. Although France is reputedly the nation in which wine is used most commonly by all segments of the population, it is actually drunk by a larger proportion of the population in Italy.

2. The quantities of wine consumed with meals in France and in Italy are approximately the same, but the use of wine between meals is substantially larger in France than in Italy.

3. Alcoholic beverages other than wine—such as beer, cider, aperitifs and especially distilled spirits—are used much more frequently in France than in Italy. It is not suggested that these other beverages are more or less toxic than wine, but the evidence is that some of them—particularly aperitifs and distilled spirits—are more

likely to be consumed on an empty stomach in the French drinking customs.

4. Early childhood exposure to alcohol is viewed differently in the two countries. Among the French, rigid parental attitudes—either strongly in favor of this childhood use or strongly opposed to it—are apparent. Italian parents, on the contrary, regard this matter un-emotionally, as a normal and relatively unimportant part of a child's development.

5. The inebriating or otherwise harmful potential of alcoholic beverages are more clearly apparent to the Italians, who set much lower "safe limits" than do the French for the amount of wine which may be taken without harm by adults and, especially, by children.

6. Among the French, there is a wide acceptance of the notion that drinking—particularly copious drinking—is somehow associated with virility. No such concept was noted among the Italians.

7. Among the French there is likewise wide social acceptance of intoxication as a humorous, fashionable or otherwise tolerable phenomenon. Among the Italians intoxication is consistently re-garded as a personal and family disgrace.

8. Among French physicians, as among Italian physicians, major emphasis is placed on the somatic aspects of excessive drink-ing and alcohol addiction. As a logical corollary, major emphasis has been placed on a fixed (although controversial) limit of alcohol consumption which cannot be exceeded with safety. In northern Europe and the United States, in contrast, increasing emphasis is being placed on the psychological aspects of alcohol abuse, and the manner of drinking and the emotional factors involved are con-sidered to be more important than the actual quantities consumed.

9. Although the death rates from alcoholism are high in France as a whole, they are far from uniform in the various regions of the country. The highest death rates are reported from those regions—especially Normandy and Brittany in the Northwest—in which wine is least frequently used, but is replaced by other alcoholic beverages, and in which drinking between meals is most prevalent. These and related factors are those that have previously been found associated with the drinking patterns of alcoholics in such countries as the United States (31, 51), Switzerland (9) and Brazil (40). In contrast, the lowest death rates from alcoholism (quite similar to those in Italy) are found in those regions—espe-

cially in the south of France—in which wine is most frequently used, along with considerable amounts of aperitifs, and in which drinking with meals is most common. These are part of the same cluster of physiological and psychological factors which were found associated with the safer drinking patterns of Italy.

10. The use of milk, fruit juices, sodas and other nonalcoholic beverages appears to be increasing in France. While their nutritional value is obvious, their possible value in directly combating alcoholism should not be exaggerated. These nonalcoholic beverages have been widely used in the United States, where the rate of alcoholism is comparatively high, but they are still relatively uncommon in Italy, where the rate of alcoholism is low.

11. Of far-reaching significance in France seems to be the growing appreciation among young men and young women of the seriousness of the problem of alcoholism, a continuing appreciation of the usefulness of alcoholic beverages but a diminishing belief that they are "essential," and at least a beginning of more moderate drinking habits and drinking attitudes.

Two observations on the comparative development of drinking patterns in France and Italy seem highly pertinent to the relative rates of alcoholism. One concerns the first remembered drinking experience. Only 13% of the French remembered it as part of a normal family meal, compared to 83% of the Italian respondents (34, *p.* 65). The importance of the first drinking experience has been pointed out by Ullman (52, 53, 54). It seems possible that the high degree of protection demonstrated by the Italians to alcoholic excesses later in life may be related to the features of their introduction to alcohol, which almost universally takes place at home, with meals, within the framework of the family. Under these conditions, it may be expected that the Italian child will adopt alcoholic beverages from the outset as a foodstuff in liquid form, to be consumed in association with solid food and in an environment marked by the mutual responsibility and affection of the family. It is interesting that in the case of the Jews, too—another group which has demonstrated the ability to drink even in relatively large quantities without serious difficulties (47)—Landman (23) as well as Snyder (47) has shown that the introduction of children to alcohol occurs also relatively early in life, at meal times and within the framework of a strong family, or during a religious ceremony in which other family members are active participants.

The final observation from the study of the development of French drinking patterns seems likewise highly significant and pertinent to the problems of alcohol in the United States and other countries: The people who later in life will turn to excessive and uncontrolled uses of alcohol usually exhibit premonitory difficulties during adolescence. In France this tendency is marked by leisure-time activities centered around alcohol, by drinking away from the moderating influences of the family, by drinking apart from meals, by attributing characteristics of virility or manhood to drinking and especially to heavy drinking, and by repeated episodes of intoxication or immoderate drinking. The relationship between adolescent behaviors and the development of excessive drinking or addiction in adult life may exist also in the United States. The hopeful trend among French youth is the growing awareness of the danger inherent in alcoholic excesses.

It has become evident to clinicians that the treatment of alcohol addiction is difficult and, at best, has thus far yielded only moderate success. The prevention or treatment of early youthful manifestations of inebriety, however, should be less difficult and amenable to an educational approach. Education in this field, we believe, should demonstrate factually the dangers not merely of addiction but of inebriety itself. But to be effective it should not be exclusively negative. Education should give appropriate recognition to the nutritional and psychological advantages of the moderate and non-inebriating use of alcoholic beverages.

It seems to us that the efforts to eradicate unsafe drinking and alcoholism can achieve a significant measure of success only if they are applied vigorously first to inebriety, for without inebriety there can be no alcohol addiction. If the cloak of social acceptance is removed from inebriety, and individuals learn to drink under physiological and psychological conditions which prevent inebriety, a major step toward the eventual prevention of alcoholism will have been taken.

Bibliography

1. ATWATER, W. O. and BENEDICT, F. G. An experimental inquiry regarding the nutritive value of alcohol. Mem. nat. Acad. Sci. 8: 235–397, 1902.
2. BASTIDE, H. Une enquête sur l'opinion publique à l'égard de l'alcoolisme. Population, Paris 9: 13–42, 1954.
3. BOE, A. DE. Les problèmes de l'alcool en Pologne. Bull. d'Informations du Haut Comité d'Étude et d'Information sur l'Alcoolisme, No. 36, pp. 3–19, 1960.
4. BRESARD, M. La consommation des boissons en France. In: Rapport au Président du Conseil des Ministres sur l'Activité du Haut Comité d'Étude et d'Information sur l'Alcoolisme. Paris; 1958.
5. BRESARD, M. L'opinion publique et l'alcoolisme. Population, Paris 3: 544–548, 1948.
6. BRESARD, M. Consommation d'alcool et mortalité par cirrhose du foie à Saint-Étienne et à Marseille. Bull. Inst. nat. Hyg. 14: 367–372, 1959.
7. DANIEL, L. J. The nutritive value of alcohol. N.Y. St. J. Med. 51: 1283–1284, 1951.
8. DAVIES, D. L. Normal drinking in recovered alcohol addicts. Quart. J. Stud. Alc. 23: 94–104, 1962.
9. DEVRIENT, P. and LOLLI, G. Choice of alcoholic beverage among 240 alcoholics in Switzerland. Quart. J. Stud. Alc. 23: 459–467, 1962.
10. EFRON, V. and KELLER, M. Selected Statistical Tables on the Consumption of Alcohol, 1850–1962 and on Alcoholism, 1930–1960. New Brunswick, N. J.; Publications Division, Rutgers Center of Alcohol Studies; 1963.
11. FLANZY, M. and CAUSERET, J. Contribution à l'étude physiologique des boissons alcooliques. Ann. Inst. nat. Rech. agron., Paris 2: 227–240, 1952.
12. HAGGARD, H. W. and GREENBERG, L. A. The effects of alcohol as influenced by blood sugar. Science 85: 608–609, 1937.
13. HAGGARD, H. W., GREENBERG, L. A. and LOLLI, G. The absorption of alcohol with special reference to its influence on the concentration of alcohol appearing in the blood. Quart. J. Stud. Alc. 1: 684–726, 1941.
14. HAUT COMITÉ D'ÉTUDE ET D'INFORMATION SUR L'ALCOOLISME. L'opinion française et les bouilleurs de cru. Bull. d'Informations, No. 39, pp. 2–18, 1960.
15. HUGUES, P. D' and LAVENIR, H. La Lutte contre l'Alcoolisme chez les Jeunes Marins-Pêcheurs Bretons. [Report presented to the Haut Comité d'Étude et d'Information sur l'Alcoolisme.] Paris; 1959.
16. INSTITUT NATIONAL DE LA STATISTIQUE ET DES ÉTUDES ÉCONOMIQUES. Variétés statistiques: la mortalité attribuée à l'alcoolisme en 1959. Bull. hebd. de Statistique, No. 635, p. 1, 1960.
17. JELLINEK, E. M. Phases in the drinking history of alcoholics; analysis of a survey conducted by the official organ of Alcoholics Anonymous. Quart. J. Stud. Alc. 7: 1–88, 1946.
18. JELLINEK, E. M. Phases of alcohol addiction. Quart. J. Stud. Alc. 13: 673–684, 1952.
19. JELLINEK, E. M. Estimates of number of alcoholics and rates of alcoholics per 100,000 adult population (20 years and older) for certain countries. In: WORLD HEALTH ORGANIZATION COMMITTEE ON MENTAL HEALTH. Report on

the First Session of the Alcoholism Subcommittee; Annex 1. World Hlth Org. Tech. Rep. Ser., No. 42. Geneva; 1951.

20. KELLER, M. American Drinking: Measures and Rates. [Lecture delivered at the Rutgers Summer School of Alcohol Studies, New Brunswick, N. J., July 1963.]

21. KELLER, M. Definition of alcoholism. Quart. J. Stud. Alc. 21: 125–134, 1960.

22. KELLER, M. and EFRON, V. The prevalence of alcoholism. Quart. J. Stud. Alc. 16: 619–644, 1955.

23. LANDMAN, R. H. Studies of drinking in Jewish culture. III. Drinking patterns of children and adolescents attending religious schools. Quart. J. Stud. Alc. 13: 87–94, 1952.

24. LE BIHAN, J. Les reconversions des productions alcooligènes; des possibilités . . . aux réalisations. Bull. d'Informations du Haut Comité d'Étude et d'Information sur l'Alcoolisme, No. 24, pp. 3–14, 1959.

25. LEDERMANN, S. Alcool, Alcoolisme, Alcoolisation; Données Scientifiques de Caractère Physiologique, Économique et Social. (Institut National d'Études Démographiques, Travaux et Documents, Cahier No. 29.) Paris; Presses Universitaires de France; 1956.

26. LEDERMANN, S., TRIVAS, J. and HONG, N. Privilège des bouilleurs de cru et internements en milieu rural. Population, Paris 13: 407–432, 1958.

27. LÉTINIER, G. Éléments d'un bilan national de l'alcoolisme. Population, Paris 1: 317–328, 1946.

28. LOLLI, G. The cocktail hour: physiological, psychological, and social aspects. In: LUCIA, S. P., ed. Alcohol and Civilization; pp. 183–199. New York; McGraw-Hill; 1963.

29. LOLLI, G., GOLDER, G. M., SERIANNI, E., BONFIGLIO, G. and BALBONI, C. Choice of alcoholic beverage among 178 alcoholics in Italy. Quart. J. Stud. Alc. 19: 303–308, 1958.

30. LOLLI, G. and MESCHIERI, L. Mental and physical efficiency after wine and ethanol solutions ingested on an empty and on a full stomach. Quart. J. Stud. Alc. 25: 535–540, 1964.

31. LOLLI, G., SCHESLER, E. and GOLDER, G. M. Choice of alcoholic beverage among 105 alcoholics in New York. Quart. J. Stud. Alc. 21: 475–482, 1960.

32. LOLLI, G., SERIANNI, E., BANISSONI, F., GOLDER, G. [M.], MARIANI, A., McCARTHY, R. G. and TONER, M. The use of wine and other alcoholic beverages by a group of Italians and Americans of Italian extraction. Quart. J. Stud. Alc. 13: 27–48, 1952.

33. LOLLI, G., SERIANNI, E., GOLDER, G. [M.], BALBONI, C. and MARIANI, A. Further observations on the use of wine and other alcoholic beverages by Italians and Americans of Italian extraction. Quart. J. Stud. Alc. 14: 395–405, 1953.

34. LOLLI, G., SERIANNI, E., GOLDER, G. M. and LUZZATTO-FEGIZ, P. Alcohol in Italian Culture; Food and Wine in Relation to Sobriety among Italians and Italian Americans. (Monographs of the Rutgers Center of Alcohol Studies, No. 3.) New Brunswick, N. J.; Publications Division, Rutgers Center of Alcohol Studies; 1958.

35. LOLLI, G., SERIANNI, E., GOLDER, G. [M.], MARIANI, A. and TONER, M. Relationships between intake of carbohydrate-rich foods and intake of wine and other alcoholic beverages; a study among Italians and Americans of Italian extraction. Quart. J. Stud. Alc. 13: 401–420, 1952.

36. MACABIES, J. Valeur Alimentaire des Vins de 8° a 12°. Paris; Comité National de Propagande en Faveur du Vin; 1951.

37. MALIGNAC, G. and COLIN, R. L'Alcoolisme. Paris; Presses Universitaires de France; 1954.

38. MORGAN, A. F., BRINNER, L., PLAA, C. B. and STONE, M. M. Utilization of calories from alcohol and wines and their effects on cholesterol metabolism. Amer. J. Physiol. 189: 290–296, 1957.

39. NEUMANN, R. O. Über die eiweisssparende Kraft des Alkohols; neue Stoffwechsel versuche am Menschen. Münch. med. Wschr. 48: 1126–1129, 1901.

40. PARREIRAS, D., LOLLI, G. and GOLDER, G. M. Choice of alcoholic beverage among 500 alcoholics in Brazil. Quart. J. Stud. Alc. 17: 629–632, 1956.

41. PERRIN, P. L'Alcoolisme; Problèmes Médico-Sociaux; Problèmes Économiques. Paris; L'Expansion Scientifique Française; 1950.

42. POPPER, K. The Open Society and Its Enemies. Princeton, N. J.; Princeton University Press; 1950.

43. RICHTER, C. P. Alcohol as a food. Quart. J. Stud. Alc. 1: 650–662, 1941.

44. SADOUN, R. and LOLLI, G. Choice of alcoholic beverage among 120 alcoholics in France. Quart. J. Stud. Alc. 23: 449–458, 1962.

45. SERIANNI, E., CANNIZZARO, M. and MARIANI, A. Blood alcohol concentrations resulting from wine drinking timed according to the dietary habits of Italians. Quart. J. Stud. Alc. 14: 165–173, 1953.

46. SILVERMAN, M. A Study of Drinking Habits. [Lecture delivered at University of California, Davis, Calif., December 1960.]

47. SNYDER, C. R. Alcohol and the Jews; A Cultural Study of Drinking and Sobriety. (Monographs of the Rutgers Center of Alcohol Studies, No. 1.) New Brunswick, N. J.; Publications Division, Rutgers Center of Alcohol Studies; 1958.

48. STOETZEL, J. Les caractéristiques de la consommation de l'alcool. In: Rapport au Président du Conseil des Ministres sur l'Activité du Haut Comité d'Étude et d'Information sur l'Alcoolisme. Paris; 1958.

49. STOETZEL, J. Le public et le problème de l'alcoolisme. In: Rapport au Président du Conseil des Ministres sur l'Activité du Haut Comité d'Étude et d'Information sur l'Alcoolisme. Paris; 1958.

50. SUTTIE, I. D. The Origins of Love and Hate. New York; Julian Press; 1952.

51. TERRY, J., LOLLI, G. and GOLDER, G. M. Choice of alcoholic beverage among 531 alcoholics in California. Quart. J. Stud. Alc. 18: 417–428, 1957.

52. ULLMAN, A. D. The first drinking experience of addictive and of "normal" drinkers. Quart. J. Stud. Alc. 14: 181–191, 1953.

53. ULLMAN, A. D. Sex differences in the first drinking experience. Quart. J. Stud. Alc. 18: 229–239, 1957.

54. ULLMAN, A. D. Ethnic differences in the first drinking experience. Social Probl. 8: 45–56, 1960.

55. U. S. BUREAU OF HOME ECONOMICS. Diets of Families of Employed Wage Earners and Clerical Workers in Cities. (Circular No. 507.) Washington, D. C.; U. S. Department of Agriculture; 1939.

56. U. S. DEPARTMENT OF AGRICULTURE. Food Consumption of Households in the United States. (Household Food Consumption Survey 1955, Report No. 1.) Washington, D. C.; 1956.

57. WILLIAMS, P. and STRAUS, R. Drinking patterns of Italians in New Haven. Quart. J. Stud. Alc. 11: 51–91, 250–308, 452–483, 586–629, 1950.

Index

Index

129

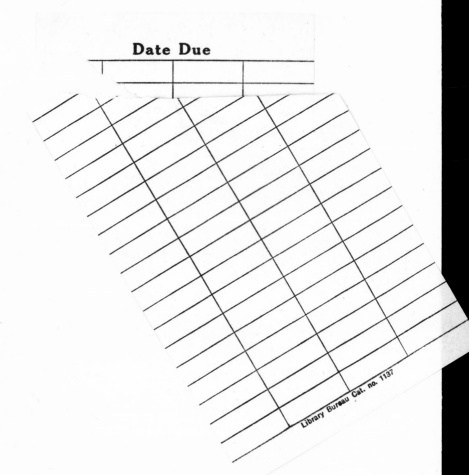

Date Due

Library Bureau Cat. no. 1137